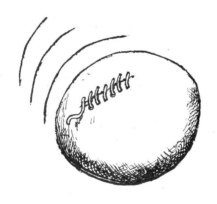

'I remember William Webb Ellis perfectly. He was an admirable cricketer, but was generally inclined to take unfair advantages at football. I should not quote him in any way as an authority...'

Mr T. Harris, in a speech to the Old Rugbeian Society.

The BOOK
-OF-
Rugby
DISASTERS
&
BIZARRE
RECORDS

GENERAL EDITOR
FRAN COTTON
INTRODUCED BY
BILL BEAUMONT
ILLUSTRATIONS BY
COLIN WHITTOCK
COMPILED BY
CHRIS RHYS

Stanley Paul
London Melbourne Sydney Auckland Johannesburg

Stanley Paul & Co. Ltd
An imprint of Century-Hutchinson Ltd
17-21 Conway Street, London W1P 6 JD

Hutchinson Group (Australia) Pty Ltd
16-22 Church Street, Hawthorn, Melbourne, Victoria 3122

Hutchinson Group (NZ) Ltd
32-34 View Road, PO Box 40-086, Glenfield, Auckland 10

Hutchinson Group (SA) Pty Ltd
PO Box 337, Bergvlei 2012, South Africa

First published by Century Publishing Co. Ltd 1984
Stanley Paul edition 1985

© Lennard Books 1984, 1985

Set in Century Schoolbook

Printed and bound in Spain by
TONSA, San Sebastian

Made by Lennard Books
Mackerye End, Harpenden
Herts AL5 5DR

Editor Michael Leitch
Designed by David Pocknell's Company Ltd
Production Reynolds Clark Associates Ltd

Cataloguing in Publication Data
Rugby disasters and bizarre records
1. Rugby football – anecdotes, facetiae, satire etc.
I. Cotton, Fran
796.33'3' 0207   GV945.2

ISBN 0 7126 0911 3 (cased)
ISBN 0 09 162821 0 (paper)

CONTENTS

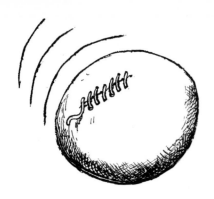

INTRODUCTION

I must say I was intrigued to learn that this book on the great disasters of rugby was being compiled by a Welshman, and presumed it would concentrate on the singular lack of success by Wales in the 1980s. No such luck. I have to admit my next train of thought led me to fear that Chris Rhys might have shifted his attention to that rather fallow period from 1963 to 1979 when

England's name did not feature all that prominently or often on the roll of honour. Happily, in this highly entertaining collection of anecdotes he has chosen a much wider canvass to explore, and the end product is essential reading for followers of the game.

My initial reaction, when asked what I thought was the greatest disaster in Rugby Union in my time, was disarmingly simple and straightforward. I have long held the view that the fact that the parents of Gareth Edwards, Barry John, Gerald Davies and Phil Bennett were not all English, and that these four bouncing babies were not born in England, was a disaster of the most monumental proportions bordering on the unforgiveable. One disaster provokes another, and so it was, while preparing for my first international against Wales in Cardiff, that I remember our coach telling the England squad at training to take up their usual positions. Imagine my trepidation as a fresh-faced youth when I saw our team jog downfield and line up behind the goal-line to wait for the conversion.

Of course, history shows that there was no great reason for England to suffer from complacency or over-confidence when confronted by Wales. Of my six internationals against Wales, five fall neatly into the pigeonhole reserved under the title of this book. However, on the other occasion, at Twickenham in 1980, we really crushed the Welsh, admittedly reduced to 14 men with the early departure of Paul Ringer, by three penalty goals to two tries. Up to that point I had often argued that the value of the penalty goal was disproportionately high, but it is amazing, in retrospect, how easily one's judgment can be clouded. Mind you, I was made painfully aware the following year down in Cardiff that one swallow does not make a summer. I found it bad enough that we lost 21–19, but the felony was compounded by enthusiastic Welshmen during the week of the match selling lapel badges to

Bill Beaumont reflects quietly on his good fortune in picking New Zealand's wettest-ever winter, that of 1977, to tour there with the Lions.

ecstatic fans swathed in red and white scarves which stated: 'Bill Beaumont walks on water', with the PS: 'Bullshit floats'.

In my first year of international rugby I experienced one of the great disasters which tend to befall most players at some time or other – playing out of position. After a tempestuous opening few minutes in the match against Australia at Brisbane, I was back in our changing room having some stitches inserted into a head wound when I heard the ominous sound of studs on concrete slowly making their way towards the door. It opened hesitatingly and in came Mike Burton. He had just been sent off, and for the only time in his whole life he was rendered speechless. He sat in silence staring at the ground as I returned to the fray. I was met on the touchline by the England manager Alec Lewis who inquired politely: 'Have you ever played prop forward before or will the next 75 minutes be your first attempt?'

My very first disaster in rugby nearly ended my career before it had begun. I promised my mother on my first away match in Durham that I would be home long before midnight. A surfeit of good beer and bad company meant that I phoned home feeling and sounding slightly the worse for wear in the early hours of the morning. As I was about to ring off I heard my mother turn to my father in bed and say: 'That's it. Bill has just played his last game of rugby.' Fortunately, I survived to take part in my fair share of rugby disasters – and with that background I am ideally placed to appreciate this book to the full and commend it warmly.

Bill Beaumont

RUGBY
WARTHOGS *AND* ALL

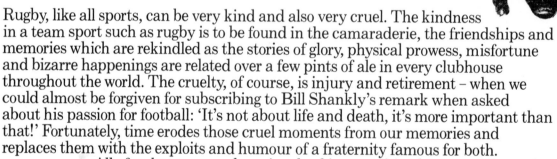

Rugby, like all sports, can be very kind and also very cruel. The kindness in a team sport such as rugby is to be found in the camaraderie, the friendships and memories which are rekindled as the stories of glory, physical prowess, misfortune and bizarre happenings are related over a few pints of ale in every clubhouse throughout the world. The cruelty, of course, is injury and retirement – when we could almost be forgiven for subscribing to Bill Shankly's remark when asked about his passion for football: 'It's not about life and death, it's more important than that!' Fortunately, time erodes those cruel moments from our memories and replaces them with the exploits and humour of a fraternity famous for both.

     All of us have seen or been involved in something bizarre on the rugby field and some of the recollections in this book, relating to games in which I personally was involved, bring home the historical significance of those incidents. Not for one moment did I realize that I was present when the first streaker was arrested at an international – on 24 March 1974 during the Air Disaster Match between England and France at Twickenham. Mind you, I would have much preferred to have been present some eight years later, when during half-time in the international between England and Australia, Erika Roe did her famous streak. Bill Beaumont, who was the England captain on that day, has contributed his recollections but I much prefer those of Steve Smith who typically was the first member of the England team to spot the delightful Miss Roe appearing from the terraces. Billy was as famous for his large buttocks as he was for his rugby ability, and when he attempted to regain the attention of his team with a final plea of 'What *is* going on?' his scrum-half quipped: 'Hey, Bill, there's a bloke jumped over the fence with your arse on his chest.'

Rugby touring has without doubt thrown up the highest incidence of disasters and bizarre occurrences. How many can say that they have had to abandon their practice game because a very unfriendly warthog invaded the pitch? Well, it happened on the 1974 British Lions Tour to South Africa during a practice held at one of the camps in the Kruger National Park. And when you realize that certain members of the touring team couldn't sleep for fear of snakes hiding in the rafters of their *rondavels*, you can imagine how keen they were to leave the field when the warthog suddenly charged on.

The excursion to the Kruger National Park in 1974 also produced another remarkable feat when Mervyn Davies broke the British Isles and Eire Rugby Union Touring Team drinking record by some considerable margin. At the time, rather like Bob Beamon's leap in the 1968 Mexico Olympics, it seemed a record which would not be broken in our lifetime, but on the next Lions tour to New Zealand, in 1977, that immense character from Kerry, Maurice Ignatius Keane, sank the record without trace. Moss, incidentally, was the first Gaelic Footballer to represent Ireland at rugby.

There are many excellent books which detail the records and statistics of this greatest of team sports. This present volume concentrates more on revealing, in a light-hearted way, the true character and philosophy of the game and its universal appeal. I hope you chuckle as much as I have done while going through this extraordinary assortment of bizarre and sometimes disastrous occurrences. No doubt they will remind you of others which you yourself have experienced or suffered.

Fran Cotton in the Lions front row with Peter Wheeler and Graham Price in the Second Test at Christchurch, New Zealand, in 1977.

MOST
UNLIKELY
VENUES

Weather vane at Twickenham, the well-known former market garden.

From the highest to the lowest, all venues seem strange to someone. When in 1907 it was proposed to make Twickenham the headquarters of the RFU, someone disdainfully wrote: 'The site chosen is a market garden. Whether Twickenham will prove to be the ideal site is very doubtful.'

Indeed, setting up a club can be the most difficult business of all. When Southwold RFC was first formed, the members applied to the council to use part of Southwold Common for a pitch, and permission was duly granted. The common is a large piece of land, between the town and the harbour, and includes a nine-hole golf course, cricket, football, and now rugby pitches. The whole area is criss-crossed with old pathways.

During the rugby club's first season, an elderly lady was seen **walking diagonally across the field of play with her dog.** Not only was she exercising her dog, she was also exercising her right to walk on common pathways. The habit became folklore, and referees were warned in advance. Play was stopped when she turned up, players welcomed her with a polite good afternoon and applauded her from the field of play. This happened for five or six seasons until she died.

Another club to launch itself in a modest way was Vigo RFC, located in the wilds of Kent between Maidstone and Gravesend and named after the pub in which someone first had the great idea, one boozy Sunday lunchtime in 1969, of starting a team. In the cold and sober light of Monday, and for several days and weeks thereafter, the beauty of the idea was much questioned. Practical matters seemed also to defy solution, such as **where to get a set of posts.**

Assuming that it was possible to buy them, even if no Vigoan knew where, the organizers sent out begging letters to any person who had ever offered to buy a round in the pub, but this brought neither joy nor cash. Eventually they decided they would have to make their own, and some diseased elms from the nearby woods were felled, trimmed and re-erected on the field loaned to the club by the landlady of the Vigo Inn.

In the early years there was no clubhouse, but if the landlady was in a reasonable mood the teams changed in the public bar after drinking-up time. If she was not, they were **banished to a large disused chicken coop** in the corner of the field.

What else does a rugby club need? Washing facilities? They had those. After a match, the worst of the mud was washed off at a free-standing tap in the field, and then each Vigo player took a visiting opponent back to his own home for a hot bath, a mug of tea and perhaps a meal, before returning to the pub for the evening. One of the Rosslyn Park sides thought this was such a charming ritual that they came back the following week when a fixture was cancelled.

A similar pioneering spirit was evident in 1972 when the Cayman Islands RFC was founded – with no ball, no pitch, and certainly no clubhouse. Their nearest opponents were in Jamaica, six hundred miles away, which may qualify them as the **most travelled and least-exercised wandering club.** However, in 1975, led by famous Golden Oldie Jeff Butterfield, the club secured the rights to hack a proper rugby ground from a patch of pine forest – which they did.

Things are different nowadays in the Caribbean. As an official of Trinidad and Tobago RFU put it, touring clubs are very welcome, especially in August. He added: 'You pay to get here… we'll look after the transportation, some entertainment, **and your laundry.'**

In the Pacific, Fiji have a long-established reputation for rugby. Their first overseas international was played against Western Samoa at Apia in 1924. The pitch contained a large tree on the halfway line which hindered kicking and called for careful negotiation. The match, which Fiji won 6–0, had to start at 7 am to allow the home players time to get to work after the game.

In 1948 Fiji played the New Zealand Maoris at Suva. This was the first time the team had worn boots, and many players complained of soreness and cramp; some wrenched off their boots and flung them across the touchline, but there was little they could do to stop the Maoris winning 24–6.

AN OLD LADY'S IDEA OF WHAT THE ALL BLACKS' FROM MAORI-LAND ARE LIKE

When the Fijians came to Britain in 1970, one or two jokers in the squad enjoyed playing up their 'primitive' background. A young agency reporter on one of his first assignments made the mistake of asking a large Fijian forward how they celebrated after their matches. 'The winners eat the losers,' he replied.

Excerpt from a Tongan handbook: 'We prefer rugby to cricket. Rugby jerseys last four years. We can't afford cricket balls, they are too expensive. Boots are a problem. The RFU forced us to wear them in 1940…'

Skirted Fijian tourist at Paddington Station in 1964, on his way to Wales.

In 1983 there were four rugby clubs in Indonesia. One came from the International Sports Club in Djakarta and was full of well-fed and slightly corpulent businessmen. Another was made up of French oil-rig workers in the Kalimantan province of Borneo. The third club, at Bandung, was chiefly noted for its ground which had a 15-foot rise between touchlines. The fourth was also noted for its ground: the club were from a US Navy vessel, and **insisted on playing their home matches aboard ship!**

In Tahiti, because of the high daytime temperatures, all rugby matches are scheduled as evening kick-offs. To prevent the afternoons from becoming tedious, all visiting teams are invited to an extra function *before* the game.

In Bahrain, the only playable turfed pitch is at the airport. Games take place alongside the main runway, and have often been halted for the arrival and departure of Concorde and Jumbo jets.

In Gibraltar they play a modified form of Rugby Union. Because there is no grass on the only pitch on the Rock, visiting teams are invited to play a form of touch rugby to avoid serious injury.

The **lowest-ever rugby match** was held on the shore of the Dead Sea, 385 m (1,286 ft) below sea level on 29 October 1982. A team from Aqaba and Safi challenged Amman on a pitch prepared by the construction company George Wimpey, who also provided half the players. The temperature was in the low 90s, and Amman, who led 6–4 at half-time, eventually won 26–10.

Action from the lowest-ever rugby match, played on the shore of the Dead Sea in 1982 between Amman (hoops) and Aqaba and Safi.

In the Far East, rugby is viewed very differently according to where you find yourself. The sport is banned in the People's Republic of China, a bulletin from their Sports Council explaining that 'the **meeting of sullied bodies in physical contact** cannot be approved. There is no place for these elements in our society.' Thus, when the Shanghai club folded in 1952 after the naval connection was virtually severed, the surplus funds were presented to the RFU for a **Royal Retiring Room** at Twickenham.

In Japan, on the other hand, rugby has been popular since the 1920s, when the Japanese RFU published a pamphlet called **'The Land of the Rising Scrum.'** The Japanese Royal Family have been patrons of the game since those early days, thanks to the efforts of Shigeru Kayama, president of the RFU, who in the course of a long sea voyage successfully marketed his enthusiasm to Prince Chichubu. Today the only sports statue in Tokyo – capital of a land of judo, sumo wrestling, baseball and gymnastics – features a scrum-capped rugby player. It stands outside the main entrance to the Olympic Stadium.

In 1964 the authorities in Yugoslavia, where they had been playing Rugby League, took the decision to tell all their clubs to stop playing the game and switch to Rugby Union! It is not known whether the Yugoslavs at that time did not like professionalism, or were unsure what game they were playing in the first place.

Mudlark at the Hong Kong Sevens in 1983: All Black Andrew Donald waits while a Samoan player digs the mud from his eyes.

Distance is a problem for members of Oslo RFC, who need around 48 hours to complete an away fixture. The pattern of a usual 'away' weekend is to catch a boat on Friday afternoon, play on Saturday and travel home again on Sunday in time for work on Monday. The only other Norwegian club is at Stavanger, a round trip of 685 miles, and the nearest club is at Karlstad in Sweden, a round trip of 310 miles. Recently, for a change, Oslo were hosts to a team of New Zealanders working on the North Sea rigs, who called themselves the Oil Blacks.

One of the more remarkable games of rugby was played at a POW camp in Poland, **withing 'smelling distance' of Auschwitz concentration camp.** The pitch was the parade ground used for roll-call and exercise, so was virtually grassless. The temperature was below freezing.

The fixture was between 'Scotland' and 'Wales' and took place on a Sunday, the rest day. Snow had fallen to a depth of ten inches the previous evening. The players stamped down the pitch. The teams took the field in ammo boots, trousers, shirts and balaclavas. The game lasted 20 minutes each way. Wales won by two tries to nil. Conversions were not attempted because balls, like players, were not allowed over the wire.

Afterwards the teams returned to their huts for a wipe-down with a blanket. After-match festivities were conducted in the proper manner. Booze was a concoction of prunes, currants, fruit, schnapps, wood alcohol, and any other available liquid.

Bad weather has blighted many a fixture, turning benign rugby grounds into unplayable boglands, snowfields, etc. **The coldest venues must be in the USSR.** On 19 October 1978, when Krasnoyarsk played Polytechnika Alma Ata, the temperature was minus 23°C. The teams wore balaclavas, gloves and tracksuits to try and shield themselves from the Siberian blast. No-one was keen to cancel the match since the visitors had travelled some 1,200 miles to get there!

The organizers of the 1890 University match had problems with the weather. The game was arranged for the Queen's Club, West Kensington, on 10 December, but on the day 'a thick fog obscured the ground' and both teams were sent home. The match was re-arranged for 18 February. The fog came down again. A third attempt was made for 25 February. The fog came down yet again. While Oxford were advised not to travel, Cambridge were already at the ground. The match was eventually played on 2 March, and finished in a 6–6 draw.

The England v Wales match of 1908, played at Bristol, was **another Fog Horror Story.** So thick was the fog that each time there was a score, players had to find their way to the touchlines to inform the crowd and shivering pressmen.

It was much the same story in November 1982, when Gloucestershire beat Surrey 19–16 in a county championship match at Gloucester. Or, at least, that is the general belief. The game was played in thick fog, the television cameras could not detect anything vaguely to do with the game, and two players were still wandering aimlessly around the pitch five minutes after the final whistle, unaware that the game had finished.

In Holland, after the severe snowstorms of 1978–79, many of the pitches were unplayable and League fixtures were rearranged to take place on the beaches. The season was completed on time.

On 12 February 1983, the game between East Peckham and Wellcome had been rescheduled for the morning so that most of the home team could go to their captain's wedding that afternoon. Unfortunately there were severe snowstorms in the night, and when the teams turned up at the ground **no pitch markings were visible.** The goal posts were white, and there were no flags on the white corner posts. East Peckham play in red and Wellcome in blue, but that day Wellcome unaccountably turned up in red also. The referee arrived in a white tracksuit and said it was too cold to take it off. He also forgot his whistle. Rumour has it that East Peckham won the match 14–6.

BIZARRE TACTICAL PLOYS

The club game at its finest: Bexhill on tour in Dieppe, complete with fattest forward, longest shorts, most prudent evasive tactics – and an opponent with an alarming line in black magic hand signals.

HOW TO GET RESULTS

Noel Murphy, coach of the 1980 Lions to South Africa:

'Right, lads, I want 80 per cent commitment for 100 minutes!'

Murphy also invented a revolutionary tactic when he said: 'Right, lads, spread out in a bunch!'

Ray Gravell, one of the best British tacklers of the last decade, was describing the fundamentals of his art. 'Get your first tackle in early,' he said, 'even though it may be late.'

Noel Murphy (right) not training very hard in New South Wales with fellow-Lions B.G.M. Wood and Rhys Williams.

How to avoid jumping at the line-out.

HOW TO TACKLE A DOUBLE-BARREL

Mick English, Ireland's stand-off, was asked to explain a vital missed tackle on Phil Horrocks-Taylor, the England fly-half, in a representative match.

'Horrocks went one way, Taylor went the other – and I was left holding the bloody hyphen.'

HOW TO BE SELECTED

Carston Catcheside, the Percy Park three-quarter who gained eight caps for England in 1924–27, had a novel way of attracting attention. After his first international trial, he wrote his name all over the bald head of one of the selectors.

It worked.

HOW TO BE POPULAR

Torquay Athletic and Devon fly-half John Poustie made a confession in 1975 that surprised his team-mates. He revealed that he had spent most of the season 'not trying' because he believed that badly beaten teams didn't buy enough beer after the match. He admitted to dropping passes deliberately and slowing down the pace of the game.

His problem was that Torquay were having their most successful season for years, with 28 wins out of 35, and 17 of them by a clear 20 points. Poustie claimed that his right-winger was spoiling life for the whole team:

'He scored seven tries in two games and was trying to beat the club record. Our last three opponents cleared the car park before I'd got a glass in my hand!'

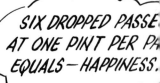

HOW TO LIE ABOUT YOUR AMATEUR STATUS

Worried about a possible defeat by Trinity College, Dublin, the weakened Cambridge University side enlisted the help of a player who had recently been recruited to the Rugby League game. The player, who was just about the opposite of academic, was told to parry any questions at the after-match banquet with 'Yes' or 'No'. This plan worked very well until his opposite number asked what subject he was studying.

'Sums,' came the reply.

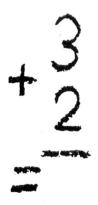

Half a dozen ways to hail a taxi.

HOW TO ANTAGONIZE REFEREES

Gareth Edwards and Barry John played together as half-backs for Wales in 23 internationals. Both came from West Wales and could speak the Welsh language fluently. This they did on several occasions to confuse the opposition. Unfortunately it also had the effect of confusing referees. Edwards and John claim that on many occasions referees misinterpreted their Welsh conversations and penalized them for swearing.

HOW TO BE REPORTED TO THE RFU

In a John Player Cup match between London Irish and Coventry in 1974, the Coventry captain was heard to say: 'Come on, Coventry, you're playing like a bunch of bloody amateurs!'

The dwarf Neary does it again.

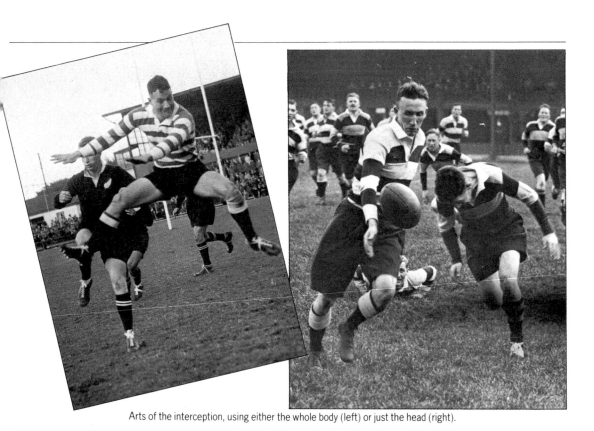

Arts of the interception, using either the whole body (left) or just the head (right).

HOW TO GIVE FORWARDS A HEADACHE

Gareth Edwards was a central figure at a Welsh team practice. Coach John Dawes had decided to introduce a couple of moves involving the back row. When the left-side flanker was to break, the codeword would begin with the letter 'P', and when the right-side flanker was involved, then the word would begin with 'S'. Dawes wanted one more practice. Edwards put the ball in and shouted 'Psychology.' Both flankers stayed down.

'Which proves not all forwards are thick,' said Dawes.

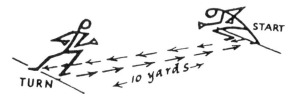

POLITICAL

T W I S T S

The Poles have been building themselves a reputation in recent years as a tricky crowd to deal with. In 1984 they had several digs at the French side due to play them in the FIRA championships. They did not want France to field either Didier Camberabero or Henri Sanz, on the grounds that they were doing their national service and might be a security risk! Yves Foulget, the Brive centre, was also an unwelcome opponent. His 'crime' was to have chosen the Armed Forces as his career.

The previous winter FIRA wanted to know why Poland had failed to fulfil a fixture with Italy. The Poles replied that they could not raise a team. 'Why not?' asked the FIRA office in Paris. **'Two of our players are dead',** came the answer. It was then revealed that one had died after a match against Romania in Bucharest, but the fate of the other man remained a mystery.

News from another source would lead us to believe that life behind the Iron Curtain can't be all bad. The Russian club Moscow Slava were on tour in Wales in 1973, and had just lost narrowly to Rhymney by 10 points to 8. One of the Rhymney supporters was warming to the social atmosphere after the game,

which had been played on a dank,
November afternoon, and suggested to a Slava player:
'Well, boyo, now's the time to defect.'
The Russian replied in faultless English:
'No, thank you, I don't like your weather.'
They have always liked their rugby in Argentina, even if the game does provoke social problems from time to time. In 1890, for instance, all 30 players and every member of the 2,500 crowd were jailed by police after a match in Buenos Aires which had been attended by President Celman. The police suspected a political meeting.
Anti-apartheid demonstrators were responsible for some **extraordinarily furtive rugby** as South African teams and their hosts struggled to complete fixtures without disruption. One of their least-publicized matches took place in September 1981, when South Africa were scheduled to play the Mid-West in Chicago. Early on the

morning of the match, while protesters were gathering, the Springboks drove 77 miles to Racine and kicked off at 9.09 am in front of 247 spectators. An hour and a half later, having won by 46 points to 12, they drove the 77 miles back to Chicago to change out of their playing kit, with the protesters unaware that the game had taken place.

There were bigger fireworks that year in Hamilton, New Zealand, where the second match of the South Africans' tour was cancelled just ten minutes before kick-off. A protester named Ellis had stolen a four-seater Cessna aircraft which he threatened to crash-land on the pitch. This did not greatly move the match organizers, who presumably reckoned they could then tow the plane away and get on with the rubgy. Then Ellis threatened to make a **suicide dive** into 300 of his fellow-protesters. The match was promptly called off.

Professionalism is still a thorny issue in the Union game, but many senior players feel that the governing bodies must show more resolve than they are doing at present. Andy Haden, the New Zealand lock-forward, has made a symbolic gesture by changing the entry in his passport relating to his occupation. This now reads 'Rugby Player'.

The medical world was deeply riven by the post-war Labour Government's decision to introduce the National Health Service. During the Hospitals Cup Final of 1946, in which St Mary's beat Guys 18–8, the National Health Act was before Parliament, and a camel, draped in a white sheet bearing the words 'BEVAN – THE LAST STRAW', was the star of the afternoon. Students in charge of the camel put the blame on a **gang of right-wing tutors** who had bribed them to demonstrate the folly of socialist medicine.

Players search for carpet tacks strewn on the pitch by an anti-apartheid demonstrator
at half-time during the match between Western Counties and
the South African tourists at Bristol in
January 1970.

Jolly flour fight at
the 1958 Hospitals Cup Final, where the riots
are just as important as the rugby.

BIZARRE
SCARS

Injuries are not funny at the time, except when they happen to match officials (see 'Bizarre Refereeing Records') or are self-inflicted. In the latter category they are still not funny if they are contrived, for instance in order to avoid taking the field against crude opposition or All Blacks (see 'Fiercest Rivals').

In the case of Steven Grabham, there is no evidence to suggest that the London Welsh centre did not intend to play against Newport in 1981–82. He was merely prevented from doing so when, on his way home from training, he **fell off Putney Bridge** into the River Thames.

Novel headgear worn in a match between Italy and France 'B'. R. Palmie of France is wearing a protective helmet . . .

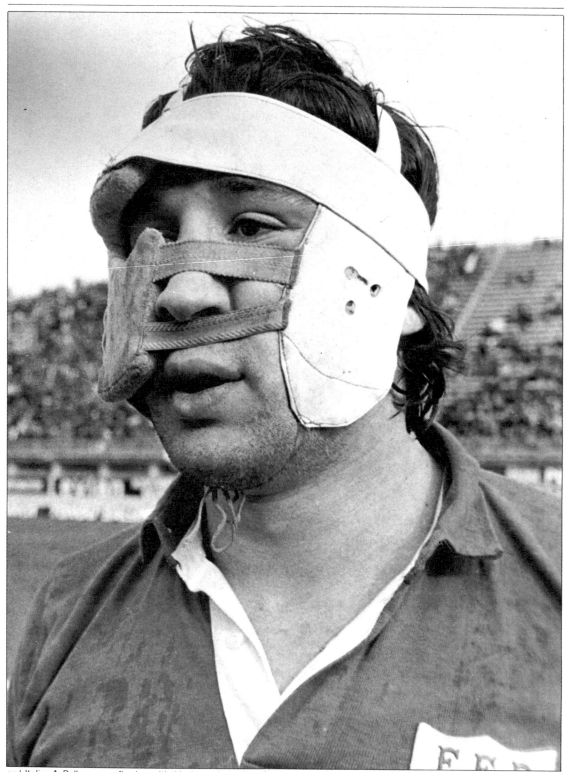

and Italian A. Bollesan was fixed up with this dramatic version of a scrum cap after sustaining a head injury.

Hugh Condon, the London Irish fly-half, was an ever-present for six years until forced to miss the Moseley match in 1984. While working in his garden he dropped a slab of concrete on his foot. As a doctor, he was able to diagnose several crushed toes *and* make out a well-argued case for not playing next Saturday.

Jean-Pierre Salut, the French international flank-forward, was proud of his selection against Scotland in 1969. The match took place at the old Stade Colombes in Paris, where the changing-rooms were under the main stand and players had to run down an alleyway and up some stairs to reach the pitch. Salut, the last man in the French team, tripped on the top step and broke his ankle. He thus became the only international player ever to be **carried off the pitch before he actually got on it.**

Tough it also was on Dickie Lloyd, the Liverpool out-half who eventually won 19 caps for Ireland, but missed out on a further cap at Belfast in 1914. He trotted out with the rest of the Ireland team to have a photograph taken before the game against Wales, then while jogging round waiting for the kick-off he suffered a muscle injury and had to be replaced.

Tony O'Reilly made a return to the international scene in 1970 for Ireland against England at Twickenham, seven years after retiring to become Chairman of Heinz. O'Reilly had been playing club rugby with London Irish to keep fit, and coped admirably with snide remarks about his chauffeur-driven Rolls and newspaper headlines suggesting that 'Beans means has-beens'. He was even gracious about being injured. What he did think a little unfair was the follow-up remark: 'Why doesn't someone kick his bloody chauffeur, an' all?'

Other mishaps taking place outside the field of play occurred to Gideon Nelson and Thomas Gisborne Gordon. Nelson was a member of the Stanford University XV which in 1924 won the last Olympic rugby championship to be contested for the United States. He was the only member of the team not to receive his medal at the ceremony: somone had **whacked him over the head with a walking stick** and he did not recover until the medals had been distributed.

Thomas Gordon's misfortune was to lose his right hand in a shooting accident at an early age. He nonetheless won three caps for Ireland in the 1870s as a three-quarter, and is thought to be the **only one-handed player** to appear in international rugby.

The South African wing J.A. Diamond suffered concussion on the field and was the victim of **'international' skulduggery** – all on the same day. Newly arrived at Oxford University in 1957–58 from Durban High School, Diamond had the misfortune to join a side captained by Peter Robbins, one of the more inventive practical jokers of his age. The team set off to play Cardiff and Diamond was asked if he had his passport with him, since he would need it to enter Wales. Not suspecting a trick, he allowed himself to be hidden in the boot of the bus, among a pile of old sacks, when it approached the border. The coach was duly 'searched' at Chepstow.

During the match Diamond was injured, suffering concussion, and was advised to stay the night in hospital. Though groggy, he was determined not to stay in a 'strange country' without his passport, so he got back on the bus, went through the same ordeal at Chepstow, and only discovered the truth when he read the story in the national newspapers shortly afterwards.

Prince Edward experienced the harder side of college rugby during the 1983–84 season. Playing for Jesus College, Cambridge against St John's, he and another player dived for a loose ball after a scrum, Prince Edward was knocked out and carried from the pitch, and ordered not to return. Without him Jesus College went from 15–6 down to 33–6 by the final whistle.

On 4 March 1984 the Abertillery centre Alun Thomas had to be helped from the field at the end of the match against Aberavon **suffering from exposure.** In a match completely dominated by forwards Thomas said that after fifteen minutes he couldn't feel his fingers. It took an infra-red lamp, several cups of tea and half an hour in the showers to revive him.

Bobby Windsor, the Welsh international hooker, had to miss the England game in 1979 having suffered severe burns the previous week caused by a council workman's lime markings on the Pontypool pitch. Windsor was burned from the top of his neck to the bottom of his spine.

Several Welsh players suffered similar agonies while on tour in Japan in 1975. Mervyn Davies, the captain, was to endure further torture when John Dawes, the assistant manager and coach, tried out a little DIY medicine. 'Lime is an acid', announced Dawes, who had once been a science teacher. 'To neutralize an acid one requires an alkali. What alkali do we have?' The remedy was near at hand: after-shave lotion. However, according to a screaming Davies, it was not a success.

There have been many **variations on the stubbed-toe theme.** Usually the victim is attempting a place-kick at the time, and the injuries range from a sore and purple big toe to a broken leg. One of the more bizarre instances occurred during England's tour of Argentina in 1936. A guest lock-forward named Frazer, from the San Isidro club, joined the England side for a charity match.

Despite his British ancestry, Frazer did not speak a word of English but this did not seem to matter at all. When England were awarded a penalty on the halfway line, Frazer trotted forward and said in Spanish: 'Give it to me. Give it to me. Let me take it'. As it was a charity match, the tourists' captain was happy to hand the ball to Frazer who quickly placed the ball, ran up, gave it an almighty clout and saw it sail between the posts.

The next time England won a penalty, the ball was promptly thrown to Frazer. This time, however, the guest player's boot hit the hard ground and he had to be carried off the field with a pulled muscle in his groin. He was given a standing ovation by the crowd, and later admitted that he had never taken a place-kick before in his life.

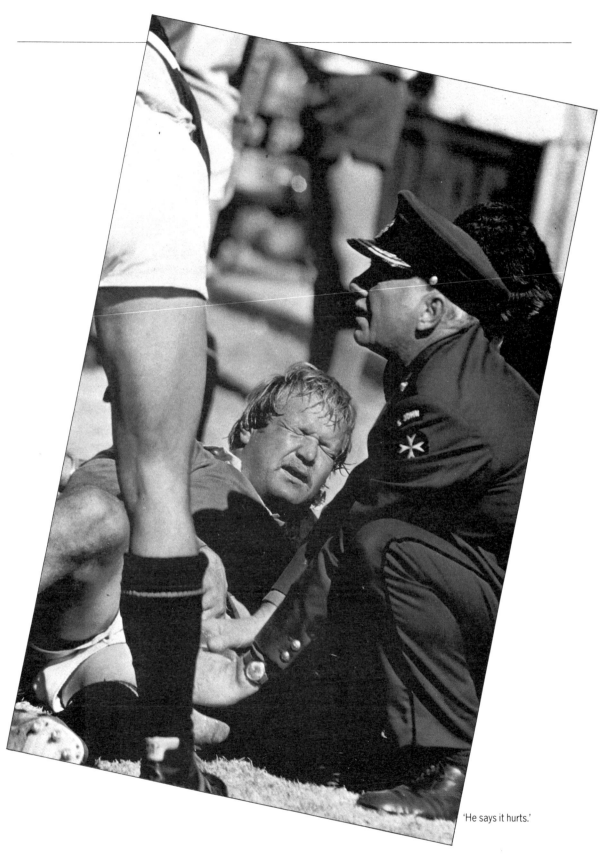

'He says it hurts.'

GAME
GIRLS

Female rugby players mostly conform to one of two images: the old and the new. Nicola Carr, a 24-year-old trainee solicitor, was one of the more old-fashioned sort, in other words she was not very good, especially when pitched in with six male team-mates to represent the Law Society in a seven-a-side tournament.

Nicola rose to the occasion, however, by scoring a try. At the time she suspected rigging by the opposition, who dived to the ground all around her, clutching thin air as she made her way to the line, stepped over one last flailing body and touched the ball down. Nevertheless, four points is four points – and Nicola was soon to make it six. As she herself described it: 'I converted the try. The ball went under the bar but the referee allowed it.'

The new image of the female rugby player is altogether different, and is being fashioned in the ranks of the under-10 mini rugby game. At Marlborough Rugby Club the winner of the award for the most improved player of the season in 1983 was Karenza Palmer, an eight-year-old girl. Nor is she alone. In a mini rugby tournament in 1981, Dartmouth beat the Cardiff side Rumney by 42 points to 4, and in the first half three tries were scored by one Toni Wilson, the Dartmouth outside-half.

At half-time there was an urgent debate in the Dartmouth camp, and as a result Toni spent the rest of the match in the pack. Later Dennis Chase, the team coach, said: 'At first I wanted to take her off at half-time because she was too good for them. The Welsh lads live for their rugby, and she was demoralizing them.'

Models full-back Claire Russell wore a hat at the 'World's Most Beautiful Rugby Match', played at the London Irish ground in 1974, in which Actresses beat Models 10–8.

Valerie Brench eludes four male pursuers and touches down for the girl students in a Men v Women charity match at South-West Technical College, Walthamstow.

All-in at the final whistle.

DISASTERS
·ON·
TOUR

If there is anything worse than suffering a disaster while on tour, it is the **disaster of not going on tour.** On the first-ever British Lions tour to Australasia in 1888, the Rugby Union sanctioned the trip but just as the ship was about to leave, representatives from HQ came aboard and took off J.P. Clowes, a Yorkshireman. They said he was already a professional. There is no record of Clowes's reaction, but he could have been forgiven for wondering why the RFU took so long to make up their minds!

More than forty years ago a certain William Pratt was secretary of the Southern California Rugby Union. He had two ambitions: one was to be a film star, and the other to arrange a rugby match between his team and England. His first wish was relatively easy to fulfil. He decided to play macabre roles in monster movies, so took the sensible precaution of changing his name from William Pratt to Boris Karloff; a star was born.

In 1938 he spearheaded a campaign to raise £10,000 to pay for a tour to England. All was going well until, a month before the tour, the treasurer vanished to South Africa with the money, never to be seen again...

Crawley RFC chose as their first major overseas tour a trip to Russia, to play five matches in ten days. Crawley raised the funds, the Russians were delighted and the Soviet Embassy in London gave its blessing to the venture. But when the Rugby Union heard of the trip they vetoed it. 'You're not big enough or good enough,' they told the Sussex club in a stern letter. Crawley stayed at home.

Then there was the **mind-boggling case of the French deportee.** In 1973 a representative team from Lorraine travelled to Cardiff to watch the Wales v France international. They had also arranged two games in Wales, and after the international they returned to their hotel to enjoy the evening in Cardiff. The following morning, one of the Lorraine team, much the worse for drink, was fast asleep in the hotel foyer. Fearing that he might miss the flight home, he was dragged out of the hotel, hustled through a bewildered and lax Customs office and put on a plane with his passport sticking out of his top pocket. The plane left for Marseilles.

Back in the hotel, the rest of the Lorraine team stumbled down to breakfast. A head-count by the captain revealed that one of their team was missing. They were then informed that their colleague was in safe hands, and was heading home on the plane, well looked after.

Spot the General Editor, having a wonderful time in New Zealand on the 1977 tour.

Sweet dreams of home, conjured by returning Lions Jeff Squire, Bruce Hay and Maurice Colclough, on the way back from South Africa in 1980.

'There are two problems,' said one of his team-mates. 'To start with, he lives in Strasbourg, which is 700 kilometres from Marseilles. Secondly, if anyone had looked, they would have found his car keys in his pocket. He drove over.'

Another form of disaster that awaits all touring sides is the **simple disaster of defeat.** The first Springbok tourists to visit Britain, in 1906–07, managed to lose twice before they even reached their destination. Gathering in Cape Town, they had some time to wait before their ship sailed so they divided themselves into two teams and played two Western Province scratch sides. They lost both matches.

The first time the South Africans toured with a springbok head as team mascot was in 1912–13. When Newport became the first side to beat them, they were presented with the head which is still on display in the clubhouse. It then became a tradition to present a head to the first side in these islands to beat the visiting Springboks.

It only needs one defeat to take the edge off an entire tour. The 1951–52 South Africans might have gone home with a 100 per cent record but for one extravagant penalty-kick. This was awarded on the halfway line late in the match against London Counties, when the tourists were leading 9–8. The kick was thumped home by No 8 forward Arthur Grumsdell, giving the home side a famous victory by 11 points to 9.

How much more frustrating must it have been for the 1974 Lions, denied their 100 per cent record in South Africa because a try was disallowed in the final minute of their 22nd and final game, which ended in a 13–13 draw.

The 1971 Lions also deserve to be remembered as one of the greatest-ever touring teams, winning their series 2–1 in New Zealand. It is no doubt churlish to recall that they lost the first game of the tour, going down 11–15 under floodlights against Queensland.

It took 67 years for a team other than the national side to beat the All Blacks in England. It finally happened on 22 November 1972, when North West Counties beat them 16–14 at Workington. Only a week later, Midland Counties West beat them 16–8 at Moseley.

The drawbacks of accepting too much hospitality were first revealed to an international touring side in the previous century. The 1896 British Lions played 21 games in 56 days in South Africa. They won 19, drew one, and lost one. The drawn match was against Western Province, in Cape Town. Before the game Dr Tommy Crean took his team to lunch at the residence of the Prime Minister, Sir Gordon Sprigg. Crean ordered that none of his team should have more than four tumblers of champagne. However, it is generally believed that none of the team took the captain's advice! They wisely turned down a return visit to the residence before the second game against Western Province, and won 32–0.

The world's worst rugby tour is claimed by a side from Basle, Switzerland, who visited France in 1974. They lost 127–0 to Grenoble, 104–3 to Thonon, and 116–0 to Annecy. They scored their only points within 25 seconds of the kick-off in their second match. From a sliced kick-off, one of the opposition players was caught offside, and the penalty hit the bar before creeping over. Captain Pierre Langlois said: 'We conceded 73 tries, I think. We even had a penalty try given against us when we were losing by over 100 points.'

Financial disaster was responsible for the inauguration of one of rugby's most enjoyable fixtures – the Barbarians versus the tourists. This match all came about because the 1948 Wallabies ran out of money and could not cover their bills. The Barbarians game was hit on as a good way to start a fund-raising exercise.

In 1984 the Barbarians themselves were in dire straits on their Easter tour to Wales, though what they lacked was points rather than cash. At one stage of their match against Cardiff they were losing 52–4, and although they recovered to lose by only 52–16, their spirits were not raised by the wag in the crowd who, at frequent intervals, was heard to yell: 'Go back to Barbaria!'

All touring sides – even sides travelling to an away fixture in their own country – would be well advised in future to consider taking an extra item of equipment with them, **namely a ball.** Thanks to the foresight of the home secretary, disaster was averted when Blantyre RFC, Malawi, undertook a tour to the island of Mauritius. When he wrote back to confirm the trip, the Mauritius secretary included the all-important line: 'Please bring your own ball. We have lost ours.'

Colwyn Bay RFC were not so fortunate. In the depths of the winter of 1966 they travelled some 50 miles across Snowdonia to play Portmadoc. All 30 players and the referee were on the field before someone realized there was no ball. A search of the club failed to produce one, nor could any contact be made with neighbouring clubs at Pwllheli and Trawsfynydd, whose fixtures had been cancelled because of the weather. So the Colwyn Bay team went home without playing.

On the Fijian tour to Argentina in November 1980, the tourists went

to Tucuman to play the regional team. During the game Senegekali, Fiji's outside-half, kicked the ball out of the ground and it was lost. A second ball was produced but was declared useless by the referee. There was no third ball, so the match had to be abandoned.

The brush with the law, an integral part of many a rugby tour, occurs with near-maximum frequency in the United States where the locals seem unable to understand the antics of rugby tourists. A member of the Letchworth club spent most of his tour in a Washington jail, after climbing the statue of Abraham Lincoln. He settled himself in Abe's lap so that souvenir photographs could be taken, but was quickly handcuffed and led away for his familiarity.

THEY DECIDED THEY DIDN'T NEED A BALL....!

Irish 'B' international Willie Anderson was detained in Argentina, and subsequently given a two-year suspended prison sentence following a representative tour in 1978. He stole the Argentine flag from one of the country's more famous monuments – a crime which carries a maximum penalty of ten years inside.

While on tour in the Heidelberg region of West Germany, three members of the Vandoeuvre Rugby Club from Nancy, France, pretended for undisclosed reasons to be ill in their hotel. An ambulance was called. The three were taken to hospital where doctors found nothing wrong with them. They were then arrested by the German police for wasting the hospital's valuable time, and this meant that they were not able to play in the next match on the tour. Vandoeuvre lost the match by 26 points to 12. Their opponents: the Heidelberg Police XV.

All that foreign travel can make players homesick. On the Welsh tour of Canada in 1973, flanker Dai Morris refused to change the time on his watch. He may have been playing in Vancouver, but he wanted to stay on Neath-time.

Are foreigners funny? Prospective opponents of Yugoslavia in the 1983–84 FIRA championships may have had mixed feelings when they learned that the Yugoslav pack contained Arsenic, in the second row, and a prop called Panic.

And so to the Japes Department. Out of the next eleven stories, eight take place in hotels, which leads us to wonder why hotel owners and managers, particularly in South Africa and the West Country, still accept bookings from touring rugby teams. However, they do, and we must be grateful to them for snapping so rarely under the inevitable strains.

On the Oxbridge tour of South Africa in 1963, a plan of attack was drawn up by the team manager Peter Robbins, aided by Roger Michaelson and Joe McPartlin, which directly involved the manager of each hotel they visited. The plan was for one or more team members to distract the manager while others stripped his room and reconstructed it in detail on the lawn outside. All went well, and harmlessly, until the tricky manoeuvring one night of a bed down eight floors finished with **the bed taking off on its own** and hurtling out into a busy Durban street.

Next day the manager called the trio into his office for an explanation. He was told that some of the younger element had enjoyed too much wine, that they would certainly be sent down from university, and the British Consul had already been involved… So moved was the manager by all this contrition and the prospect of such awful penalties hanging over the team, that he did a complete about-face and told Robbins & Co that it was quite all right really – in fact it was the done thing on a rugby tour!

The 1968 Lions had an eventful tour to South Africa. One evening two members of the touring party were returning to their hotel, the old colonial-style Pretoria Union Hotel. One of them stopped to relieve himself behind a palm tree. The other thought this was indecent, and threw a newly presented cigarette lighter in his colleague's general direction. **The tree caught fire.** This impressed both players so much that they set fire to the entire row. Said one of them later: 'It looked like a dirty great birthday cake.'

Food at last. David Hay carves the tourists' roasted pig at a barbecue in Auckland.

South African propaganda in Durban, 1980.

The 1974 Lions went on their traditional rest in the Kruger Park after a magnificent win in the Second Test in Pretoria. They travelled in two planes. One plane contained the players, the other contained the liquid refreshments calculated to cater for their few days off. The 'booze plane' ran out so quickly, it had to be sent back to base for a refill within eighteen hours of arrival.

One of the stranger injuries suffered on the 1974 Lions tour happened to the unnamed player who convinced a lady at the team's hotel in Stillfontein that he was the finest thing since sliced bread. They went upstairs, then after some time there was a knock on the bedroom door. The lady decided that it must be her husband. At this the Lion leapt out of a first-floor window, and, though he landed badly, **managed to punch a St Bernard dog** which might have revealed his whereabouts. He limped back into the hotel half an hour later, claiming he had slipped on a rock while out for a walk. He then found that the knocking had come from his room-mate, who had wanted a handkerchief and anyway had grown tired of shuffling around in the corridor while waiting to reclaim his bed.

The scene shifts to New Zealand. On the British Lions tour of 1977, some of the players decided to organize a **daffodil-eating competition.** The two finalists were the Welsh hooker, Bobby Windsor, and the Irish flanker Sean McKinney. The winner was deemed to be McKinney because while both managed to eat their supply of daffodils, McKinney had also consumed a rubber plant. Both were described as feeling a little low for the next few days.

Closer to home, about thirty players and supporters of Oldham RFC caused £1,000 damage to the Westerleigh Hotel in Torquay in April 1984. Said owner Ray Lott: 'They lost 62–0 to Exeter and I think they were a little upset!' The club repaid the debt.

Gary Winkler, hotelier of the Barrington Hotel, Paignton, threw 33 members of Otley RFC out of his hotel for unruly behaviour. Mr Winkler **heard the bar grill being opened,** phoned the police, and ordered the players off the premises. They spent the night in the team coach.

Not all rugby visitors are unquenchable looters. Some, indeed, are more sinned against than sinning. In April 1972 the Streatham and Croydon 1st XV travelled to Wales for a match and were soundly beaten by 32–3. When they arrived a little dejectedly back in their changing room they found that their valuables bag had been stolen, containing wallets and credit cards to the value of £800. It was no consolation to them that their opponents were the South Wales Police!

The 1973 All Black Mark Sayers, not the world's greatest trainer but one of the world's great pranksters, was almost singlehandedly responsible for the appalling mess in a baroque and famous Paris hotel. Having caused chaos downstairs, Sayers went back to his room and barricaded himself in for fear of retribution. Although the door held against the inevitable counter-attack, water and various implements were forced through the cracks and eventually the room was **reduced to looking like a bomb site.** The hotel manager could speak no English, but was apparently satisfied with the explanation that Sayers was also a film star back home, and had been preparing his room for a sequence for the film *The Straw Dogs!*

After the misdemeanours of the 1972–73 tour, the New Zealand

British tourists acclimatize by training next to an Australian rubbish dump, after their scheduled training ground was flooded.

touring teams were warned against future misbehaviour. Pranks were still allowed, but damage to property strictly forbidden. In 1980 in Wales, manager Eric Watson reminded his squad of the new rules. But before leaving his room to address the team, he had **forgotten to turn off his bathroom taps.** Water dripped, then poured through the ceiling on to a wedding reception below and totally disrupted the function.

Welsh internationals Mike Roberts and Glyn Shaw were room-mates in the Voyagers team at the 1973 Amsterdam Sevens. Shaw got lost in the later stages of the evening, and 'borrowed' a motor cycle to get back to his hotel.

'I didn't mind him bringing the bike back', said Roberts, 'but I drew the line when he threw my clothes out of the wardrobe and tried to park the bike in there…'

IMMORTALIZED *IN* **PRINT**

We think we know what Eddie Budgen, in all sincerity, meant. It is just that his swinish audience saw things differently. Eddie was outside-half of Imperial College, London 1st XV and also coach to the College Ladies XV. Speaking about his ladies, he was later reported as saying: 'I think the hardest thing is to get them dirty. They don't like getting on the floor. But it isn't hard to persuade them...'

IMPERIAL COLLEGE
LADIES XV

COACHING

TODAY - GETTING
THE OPPOSITION
DOWN.

Programme misprints are something most players have learned to live with. However, after scoring the only try of the game in Wales's 18–9 victory over Ireland in February 1984, Robert Ackerman may have wished to **throttle the printer** who converted his club from London Welsh to London Irish! More spectacular was the misspelling of Colm Tucker's surname in the France v Ireland programme in 1980.

On the ball

Among the pen portraits in the brochure for the London Welsh 1982 tour to the United States was the following:
'Mansell Wheelhouse
Occupation: Proof corrector with Sunday Times
Has been active member of London Wlesh since...'

In 1966, Argentina were given the nickname 'The Pumas'. In fact they should have been called 'The Jaguars'. A journalist reporting the game between Rhodesia and Argentina mistook the motif on the Argentine jersey. The name has stuck ever since.

In 1974 the *Yorkshire Evening Post* reporter phoned through his story on the Headingley v Leicester game. As he told it:
'Headingley were denied a further score when the referee missed a palpable trip on Ian McGeechan as the centre burst through.'

As it appeared in the paper: 'Headingley were denied a further score when the referee, Mr Palpable Tripp, missed a trip on Ian McGeechan as the centre burst through.'

RUGBY
DINNERS
AND OTHER
SOCIAL
DISASTERS

The mythology of rugby dinners grew a little after the France v England game in 1982. What exactly happened at the after-match banquet is still unclear. At the centre of the controversy was the Newport and England prop Colin Smart, and what he **did or did not do with the bottle of after-shave lotion** that he and the other members of the team had received from the French Federation.

Many reports insisted that, still excited by the brilliant pass he made during the game (setting up John Carleton's try), he drank a victory toast in after-shave and promptly collapsed. Certainly, he was taken to hospital. The team-doctor said: 'We had got through the hors d'oeuvres and curried saddle of lamb when Colin collapsed.'

Smart had a different version: 'I didn't eat on the day of the game, then celebrated with a rare glass of champagne. I flaked out. Part of it must have been shock at handling the ball for the first time this season.'

Police were called to break up a rowdy annual dinner held in 1935 by the CA San Isidro club in Argentina. They had particular trouble in subduing a rather large man who sorted out half a dozen officers before surrendering. It was later pointed out that the belligerent rugby player was Rafael Iglesias, the 1928 Olympic heavyweight boxing champion...

Matters did not end there. The police could not help noticing that several players were **enjoying their dinner in the nude**, and when this was reported the club was ordered to disband immediately.

M.Georges Pompidou, the French President, was not one of the world's most lively after-dinner speakers. After France had beaten Wales 12–3 in 1973, M. Pompidou was firing away on all cylinders at the post-match banquet. The players, having had quite enough of him for one evening, persuaded the Dax town band – who always play from the stands during internationals, and who were having a drink in the bar outside – to make their presence felt. In they marched, and the dinner disintegrated into good-humoured chaos.

Cliff Morgan, the former Welsh international fly-half, went to a sports forum in his later role as TV commentator and BBC Head of Outside Broadcasts. He asked for questions from the floor.

'Got one for you, Mr Morgan,' said a voice from the audience. 'Who scored the winning try for Wales against England at Twickenham in 1933?'

Various names were suggested, and each time the man shook his head. Cliff and his panel gave in.

'I bloody did!' said the questioner, and trudged out into the night.

Prince Andrew made his first public speech at the Centenary dinner of the Oxford and Cambridge rugby matches in 1981. He included the story about the cannibal youth who found a lovely girl and asked his dad if they should take her home for dinner. Father said: 'No, take her home, but **eat Mother instead**.'

In the late 1960s the committee of Slough RFC decided to invest in a colour television to encourage members to stay in the bar for a few drinks and watch *Rugby Special* later in the evening. As at many grounds, the clubhouse is in a fairly remote location. Vandals broke in and stole the television set. Slough bought another but that, too, disappeared the way of the first. After the third set had vanished, the club were advised to buy a safe and put the TV inside it. The following week, the vandals arrived and took the safe, with the contents inside. Then, mercifully, *Rugby Special* was moved to Sunday afternoons.

When Fleetwood Police were called to a local rugby club in October 1980 to quell an over-noisy party, they were surprised to discover that the ringleaders were the touring USA women's rugby squad. In 1911, the treasurer of Ireland's international XV was **all too familiar with the sounds of mayhem and breaking glass**, and wrote this pathetic note to the selection committee: 'Sirs,
… Little money is available and matches tend to be excessively expensive … our additional expenses include an escapade in a waxworks which cost us £50, whilst a ceremony known as 'Highland Honours', viz. smashing champagne glasses and bottles against a wall of a dining room, which was covered with mirrors, cost us over £80. May we give these gentlemen a cap and tell them to stay at home?'

Tonbridge RFC proudly claim the introduction to Britain of the **'Wibbely Wobbely' game.** The idea is for two teams to line up, then the first men each down a pint, pick a hat off a stump and run to another stump twenty yards away. On reaching the second stump, competitors place their already giddy heads on the top of the stump, and circle it as quickly as possible ten times. Then they set off back to the first stump, and pass on to the next man in the relay.

It's easy to explain, but less easy to do. Tonbridge eventually banned players from the indoor version after a disastrous month which produced two broken fingers, a broken collar bone and a broken nose, as contestants reeled away from their stumps. Moved outside, the game attracted further disapproval when one unfortunate, trying to regain his equilibrium, tripped over a parked motorbike and broke his ankle.

FIERCEST
RIVALS

The Pontypool front row . . . like being eaten by a fifty-stone lobster.

The competitive spirit seems to have arrived in New World rugby slightly ahead of the ability to play the game at top-class level. When England toured the United States in 1982, team members were greeted by this severe message scrawled on a dressing-room wall at the Pacific Coast Rugby Club: 'Defeat is a whole lot worse than death, because you have to live with it.'

Perhaps the Americans' own brand of football is to blame for getting them so overheated. Elizabeth Taylor, when Mrs Richard Burton, offered a balanced and cosmopolitan view: 'I prefer rugby to soccer,' she said. 'It's more like American Football which I grew up on. I enjoy the controlled violence of rugby except when they **bite each other's ears off**.' (Richard Burton, by the way, as Richard Jenkins, played for the Welsh Schools and had a season with Aberavon 1st XV before taking to the stage.)

Another commentator who came down heavily in favour of rugby was Henry Bahia – who admittedly had connections with Baltimore RFC. In 1972 he wrote:

'Rugby is a beastly game played by gentlemen
Soccer is a gentleman's game played by beasts
And American Football is a beastly game played by beasts.'

Some say the Welsh take their rugby with an **overdose of gravity.** The intense rivalry between Cardiff and Swansea was well established in 1922, when a local newspaper collected these clashing opinions:

Swansea supporter: 'The Cardiff club committee are a jealous scheming lot. The county team can well afford to dispense with such a club in which bounce, bunkum and conceit are rampant.'

Cardiff supporter: 'Cardiff players play a careless game of swift movement, sure passing and dazzling improvisation. That is beyond Swansea.'

A deadly tackle, with Terry Holmes the man in danger.

At the time of writing, investigations continue into a friendly match played at Bridgend in January 1984 between two teenage teams which ended after just eight minutes. In that time five players had been injured, and the referee felled with a broken nose.

New Zealand teams are seldom gracious in defeat, particularly while the match is still in progress. One of the fiercest matches on record was between Canterbury and the British Lions at Christchurch in 1971. The Lions won 14–3 to remain unbeaten after 11 matches, but excessive violence on the part of the opposition meant that Mike Hipwell, Sandy Carmichael and Ray McLoughlin took no further part in the tour.

Under-sixes show little mercy
in a barefoot exhibition match staged before the British Lions played Hamilton in 1977.

Thoughts on his personal safety must have gone through the mind of Earle Mitchell, the Scotland lock confronted with the task of marking the mighty Colin Meads in the All Blacks v Scotland international in 1967. Meads, the most feared and respected forward in world rugby, was seen engaged in earnest conversation with Mitchell after a line-out, and threatening all kinds of mischief. Suddenly Meads disengaged himself from throttling the young Scot and returned to the game. After the match, the conversation in the Scottish dressing-room went something like this:

'What happened there?'
'Oh,' said Mitchell, 'he was no problem. I told him to bugger off.'
'You did what?'
'Aye, I told him to bugger off.'
His team-mates clearly didn't believe him. After a moment's pause, Mitchell added: 'I did tell him to bugger off, but I must admit I didn't say it very loud.'
Opponents of the All Blacks can always console themselves with the

knowledge that the violence is not, as such, personal, and that New Zealander does it to New Zealander when there are no foreigners to play with.

On the way back from their 1924 – 25 tour to Britain, the All Blacks stopped off for two games in Canada. Four weeks of visiting the sights had left them short of match fitness.

'We thought we had better get in a bit of practice,' reported the flanker Jim Parker later, 'but we may have been too energetic.'

There were **six casualties in the practice game,** including Jock Richardson who broke a leg. The Vancouver team, who had spies present, all mysteriously dropped out of the next game.

Full-grown New Zealanders do the haka war-dance before a Welsh audience in 1980.

Even in the same family, rugby rivalry can be intense. The Bedell-Sivright brothers, Cambridge and England forwards of the early 1900s, fell out after a rugby incident. They played rugby together right through their school and university careers, but were reputed to speak to each other only once a term, on the last day, when the older would say to the younger: 'Fetch a cab home.' Silence would then be maintained until the end of the next term.

Too much rivalry can lead to victimization – or 'lots of their chaps picking on just one of ours', as it used to be called. In the 1920s former England captain Wavell Wakefield got increasingly fed up with two opposition players who were constantly kicking one of his Harlequin colleagues in a club match at Twickenham. In the end he went up and remonstrated with the two villains who immediately apologized when they saw they had been kicking an innocent player. They, apparently, had been under the impression that they had been kicking Wakefield!

Few rivalries have been as consistently intense as those between the

RFU and the Rugby Football League or Northern Union as the breakaway group named itself after the Great Schism of 1895. In 1900 a notice on the board at Northampton's ground at Franklin Gardens read:

'The committee do not hold themselves responsible for the personal safety of Northern Union agents.'

Early rugby was characterized by firmness and vigour, and Ireland's first-ever victory, against Scotland in 1881, was nothing if not hard-won. In this excerpt from a report of the match, chance favoured the Scots:

'They commenced fiercely but when Spunner and 'Big' Jock Graham had gotten black eyes, and a certain Scotsman had come out second best in an **impromptu boxing match** with David Browning, milder methods were adopted. No tangible score was made in the first half, but in the second M'Mullen of Cork making a miss catch of a long kick, placed the whole Scottish team onside: and Graham, who was leaning against the Irish goalpost, rubbing his shin after a recent hack, touched the ball down ...'

A tackle to bring tears to the eyes in a 1939 match between Rugby School (white) and Stowe.

The rivalry of place-kickers was graphically demonstrated in 1958 by French full-back Michel Vannier during a trial match at the Stade Colombes. In the Possibles team was the young aspirant Pierre (not to be confused with Claude) Lacaze of Lourdes, who was given a conversion kick in front of the posts. Vannier, with a fine disregard for the convention of charging down the kick, practised his own distracting tactic by peeing dead-centre between the posts. Lacaze ignored the **temptation of slamming in a low one** and struck the ball high over his rival's crossbar.

MOST CRUSHING DEFEATS

The highest British score is 174–0 by 7th Signal Regiment v 4th Armoured Workshop REME on 5 November 1980 at Herford, West Germany. Scores of 200 or more points have been recorded in school matches, an example being Radford School's defeat of Hills Court by 200 points to nil in 1886. Hills Court conceded 38 tries during the match.

Around the world, these are some of the heaviest defeats on record:

Europe	Comet 194	Lyndo 0 (Copenhagen, 1973)
South Africa	Ammosal 160	Kimberley Defence 6 (1977)
New Zealand	Ponsonby 2nd XV 164	Derlasal Gold 0 (1974)

In England, the record score in a cup match was registered in 1977 by Old Askeans in the Kent Cup when they beat Bredgar 150–0. The highest score in a full international was when France beat Spain 92–0 in March 1979 at Oloron. Major touring sides have also hit the high spots on several occasions. In 1962 the All Blacks beat Northern New South Wales 103–0 at Quirindi, then in Adelaide in 1974 the New Zealanders won by 117–6 against South Australia. The British Lions' best effort at mega-scoring is their 97–0 victory against South West Districts at Mossel Bay, South Africa, in 1974.

Fiji were expected to win the rugby tournament in the 1969 Pacific Games at Port Moresby. The trouble was, they found it all rather too easy, beating New Caledonia 113–13 and the Solomon Islands 113–3.

The Gordonians Club, from Aberdeen, made a return journey of over 300 miles to fulfil a Scottish premier championship fixture in 1982–83 against Hawick. They were beaten by a record 102 points to 4. Seven days later Gordonians had to make another 300-mile round trip to play Gala. Gala improved on the one-week-old record by beating Gordonians 112–4.

The South Wales Police team enjoyed a marvellous 1983–84 season, with international selections and a record points tally. But four years earlier referees had admitted blowing the whistle early to avoid unnecessarily heavy defeats. Bridgend were leading 54–9 when the final whistle was blown ten merciful minutes before time, and against Llanelli the game was ended seven minutes early

with the score reading: Llanelli 106 Police 6. Chairman Norman Chapple refused to knuckle under. 'We've had a few problems,' he said. 'We are not to be written off, though. We'll soon be a force to be reckoned with.' How right he was.

Just across the border, in the Forest of Dean, they meet this kind of calamity with unruffled understatement. As Yorkley's 1983–84 skipper Les Minchen said, after his team had been beaten 136–0 by Berry Hill: 'We are struggling to find our best form this season.'

When all your team-mates triumph, it can be hard to miss out on the fun. In 1973 Droitwich High School beat Bishop Perowne School, Worcester by 112 points to 0. Fourteen of the Droitwich team scored tries. The only player failing to register a score was the lock-forward Alex Inglis, who despite promptings from his team-mates was tackled a foot short of the line in the last seven seconds of the match.

But is it such fun after all? On the annual Easter tour to Wales in April 1982 the Barbarians were leading Penarth by 84 points to 16. At this point the Barbarians captain, David Johnston, asked the referee to stop the match five minutes early. Said Johnston: 'We were scoring at will and there's no fun to be involved in a game like that.'

LAST FOUR-POINTER

'Nim' Hall scored drop-goals for England against Wales and Scotland in 1947. He did not know it at the time, but he became the last player to score 4-point drop-goals in an international.

MONSIEUR DROP

When France beat Ireland 23–6 in 1960 to share the championship with England, Pierre Albaladejo became the first player to score three drop-goals in an international, and was subsequently nicknamed 'Monsieur Drop'. His feat was equalled in 1967 when Australia visited Twickenham and recorded a 23–11 victory, with three drop-goals by outside-half Phil Hawthorne.

MOST SPACED-OUT GOAL

In a match between RAF Cosford and Bridgnorth Colts a few years ago the Bridgnorth fly-half, Tim Webster, had just scored a try when the security police suddenly rushed on the field. At the side of the pitch was an object which they suspected was a terrorist bomb, and the players had to leave the area immediately. They then walked one and a quarter miles to the airbase's other pitches where Webster proceeded to convert his earlier try.

LOWEST DROP-GOAL

In 1972 Ian Robertson, the former Scottish international outside-half, was captain of the Public School Wanderers XV which played against Kodak. At the start of the game the Public School Wanderers only had 11 players and, as Kodak had 14, the Wanderers asked if they might borrow a couple of the Kodak team's replacements. Their request was refused, so the Wanderers took the field with eight forwards, a scrum-half, an outside-half and a full-back. They took the lead after five minutes. Robertson, with nobody to pass to, was forced to make an attempt at a drop-goal. The ball hit an upright which immediately started to collapse. In the chaos the ball rebounded to Robertson who, with the bar now no more than two feet from the ground, proceeded to drop a goal. It took 15 minutes to repair the post, by which time three of the missing Wanderers team turned up. The final score was a win for the Wanderers by that solitary drop-goal to nil.

MARATHON MATCH

On 25 April 1981, Selly Oak and Old Griffinians played a marathon rugby match. It lasted 6 hours 14 minutes, and was made up of six 60-minute periods with five-minute breaks, plus injury time. The game was controlled by four referees, and three players went off with exhaustion. The final score was a win for Selly Oak by 16 goals, 17 tries and 1 penalty (167 points) to 5 goals, 6 tries and 2 penalties (60 points).

MOST IMMORAL DEFEAT

When New Zealand beat the Lions 18–17 in the First Test of 1959 even the partisan New Zealand fans had mixed feelings. The Lions had played a sparkling brand of rugby and ran in four tries, but were beaten by six penalty goals from the boot of Don Clarke.

MOST PNEUMATIC WINNER

From Vigo, the Kent team born in a public bar (see 'Most Unlikely Venues') came that rare attacking ploy known as the Gloucester Gut Pass. Its inventor, Dave Pugh, was a corpulent prop-forward who had come up from Gloucestershire to live in the area. One day, after taking a short rest, he found himself alone in unfamiliar territory out on the wing when one of his centres made a break and suddenly had only one man to beat. Pugh decided to lend what support he could and chugged after the centre. This greyhound was now beginning to tire after a dash of some forty yards so he passed to Pugh. The problem was that all Pugh's concentration had been directed towards actually running. He did not see the ball, which, fortunately for him and for the history of rugby tactics, rebounded off his middle and flew straight back to the arms of the centre. This completely wrong-footed the opposing full-back and the centre jogged over the line for his four points.

MOST AND LEAST PROLIFIC TRY-SCORERS

The world record for tries is held by Alan Morley of Bristol, with 420 to the start of the 1984–85 season. The record, at the other end of the scale, may be held by the Old Edwardians prop Oliver Jones, who accumulated just three tries in a career of 45 seasons. His third and last try, on 15 October 1966, was scored in the same way as the other two. Jones, then aged 60, fell on the ball in the in-goal area. Apparently, Jones started playing rugby because he couldn't find anything else to do on a Saturday.

WORLD'S LONGEST TRY

The world's longest try was scored by a team from the Powerhouse RFC, Victoria, Australia. They ran the ball around Albert Park Lake, Victoria, from 4–13 March. There were no knock-ons, or forward passes, and the ball was touched down in the proper manner. The distance covered was 1,470.6 miles.

INTERNATIONAL ACES

In 1907, when England beat France 41–13, Douglas Lambert scored a record five tries. In his final international against France in 1911 he went out in a blaze of glory by scoring 22 points (2 tries, 5 conversions and 2 penalty goals) in a 37–0 victory.

In 1925, Ian Smith set an extraordinary record when he scored four tries in successive games for Scotland against France and then also against Wales.

In 1962, Michel Crauste who played 62 games for France, including 43 against Board countries, scored a hat-trick of tries from wing-forward when France beat England 13–0.

In 1978, when Australia beat New Zealand by a record 30–16 at Auckland, back-row forward Greg Cornelsen scored a record four tries.

BEST LOSER

Carles 'Hasie' Versfeld became a national hero in South Africa in 1891. He was the only player to score a try (then worth 1 point) against the touring British Lions, who won all 19 matches and scored 224 points to 1.

ONLY INTERNATIONAL NO-TRY

Jack Arigho probably scored the only no-try in international rugby. In 1929 the spectators spilled out on the field at Lansdowne Road during the game against Scotland. Arigho ran through the Scottish defence only to be confronted by a solid mass of spectators. He put the ball down in front of the fans, but the referee refused to give a try as the ball was grounded in front of the line; Scotland went on to win 16–7.

MOST MYSTERIOUS STRANGER

Local advice given to members of the Llantwit Major 3rd XV visiting Neath Athletic in March 1984 to play their 4th XV suggested that the home side's full-back was very suspect. It seemed that he had not played since his schooldays some sixteen years earlier and couldn't kick the ball. The full-back in question managed, nevertheless, to convert six tries in a heavy Neath victory. His name: John Toshack, the former Wales and Liverpool soccer player.

MOST COSTLY MISS

Two candidates are in line for this award; both committed the same sin. One is Gary Cuthbert, the Harrogate full-back, who crossed the try-line against Otley in the last match of the season. In order to make the conversion more simple, he made his way towards the posts, only to slip and put his foot over the dead-ball line. Harrogate, 6–9 down, eventually drew 9–9, but with Cuthbert's try would have won the game *and* saved their place in the Northern Merit table. Alas, they lost it.

The other transgressor was the Reverend Edward Baker who, playing for England against Ireland in 1896, went clear of the Irish defence with the scores level, but in trying to go behind the posts he too crossed the dead-ball line and so the try was disallowed. Ireland then hit back to win the game. A case of unanswered prayers?

MOST ELUSIVE BALL

There is reference in the book *One Hundred Years of Newport Rugby* to a 'record' try in the 1877 match between Rockleaze and Newport. The match was played on Clifton Downs, and there was no dead-ball line. C.B. Cross, the Newport winger, chased a long kick ahead, which went over the try line. The ball kept rolling, and Cross kept following. The ball ran downhill, and did not stop until it had crossed the main road. Cross touched the ball down 300 paces from the posts.

Many sports have their 'ball stuck in tree' stories, and rugby is no exception. At Builth Wells, Mid Wales, the visiting full-back kicked the ball into the branches of a tree which overhung the pitch. There it stuck. A spectator wandered off to collect a new ball while the players sat and rested in the sun. After a short while, the ball fell out of the tree and was caught by a member of the home side who ran on to score under the posts. To everyone's amazement, the referee awarded a try, because the ball 'under local rules, had not gone out of play'.

INTERNATIONAL
HITS
&
MISSES

The history of international rugby is strewn with bizarre feats and records. Most relate to individuals rather than teams – though teams also have their place – and the biggest category of all concerns players who nearly but not quite played for their country or the British Lions, or who played once and were never asked again, or, in the case of Bert Solomon of Redruth, played once for England in 1910 and declined all further offers of caps, preferring to play solely for his club.

First, we have an extraordinary mixed bag to sort through of **strange names, mascots, time-servers, multi-sport internationals and a few weird one-offs.** In the category of names, it must have been inevitable that a player would one day come along whose surname matched his country. Who was he?

There are two correct answers. In 1876 John Ireland played for Ireland, and Ken Scotland turned out for Scotland between 1957 and 1965.

Who is the longest-named international? We think it is the South African Willem Ferdinand van Rheede van Oudtschoorn Bergh. Widely known as Ferdie, he gained 17 caps between 1931 and 1938.

Caps flew thick and fast in 1967–68. During that season the four home countries and France used 137 players in the championship. Wales selected 30 players including 13 new caps, England 28 (11 new caps) and Scotland 26 (11 new caps).

Quite a few club sides nowadays field a handful of internationals, but we believe the Newport team that played Bristol in 1921 was unique in being all-international, with three Englishmen, one Scot, one Irishman and ten Welshmen.

When it comes to producing specialists, Heriot's FP can almost claim to have **cornered the market in Scottish full-backs.** Since Dan Drysdale in 1923, they have supplied the national side with J.M. Kerr, T. Gray, I.H.M. Thompson, Ken Scotland, Colin Blakie, Ian Smith and Andy Irvine.

Awards for longest-serving international go to the Scot W.C.W. Murdoch, who won his first cap in 1934–35 and finished with four in 1947–48; to Englishman Jack Heaton of Waterloo, who was first capped in 1934–35, and finally in 1947; and to Welshman Haydn Tanner who won the first of his 25 caps in 1938 and the last in 1949.

England's **most golden oldie** is L.E. Saxby. When he was called up to play for England against South Africa in 1931 he had been playing club rugby for more than 20 seasons. He won a second cap that season, against Wales, and at well over 40 years of age he is England's oldest-ever international. No-one knows quite how old he was at the time since there is no record of his birth date – so his record will be hard, if not impossible, to beat.

Eric Evans is another record-holding English golden oldie. His feat is that of being the first international to play against successive touring sides from overseas. He played against the 1947–48 Australians and he played them again in 1957–58.

Contrast L.E. Saxby's slow and stately rise to the top with the meteoric progress of Ian Smith. He began the 1968–69 season in London Scottish 3rd XV and on 6 December turned out for Scotland against South Africa. (The parallel zoom to fame of Mervyn Davies – in the same season – is recorded in another chapter, 'Fit For Nothing'.)

England's **luckiest human mascot** was W.J.A. Davies. He played in 22 matches for his country and was on the winning side in all his 21 home

internationals; his only taste of defeat was against South Africa in 1913. Davies partnered Cecil Kershaw at half-back in 14 internationals, and in all 14 they were winners.

As for successful teams, one of the best and perhaps the unluckiest were the New Zealand touring side of 1924–25 who played 32 matches in Britain, France and Canada and won them all. They were only deprived of an international grand slam by Scotland, who before the tour decided that a match against New Zealand would draw few spectators and be a financial disaster. Despite this piece of Scottish eccentricity the tourists became known as 'The Invincibles'; New Zealand, however, had to wait until 1978 for their grand slam.

Also under-rated by some (or most) observers were the England side who toured South Africa in 1972 after being totally whitewashed for the first

time in the five nations championship. **Spurred by this record run of defeats,** they won six matches in South Africa and drew the seventh – and beat South Africa in the only Test.

One year earlier, the British Lions returned home in glory after their first-ever series victory in New Zealand. Back in England it was summer, and the Lions agreed to play in a charity cricket match in South London. They were bowled out for just 14 runs and the game was over inside an hour!

Family connections are not all that common at international level, but certain brothers have left their mark – Billy Bancroft literally so, when against England at Cardiff in 1893 he became the first player to drop a goal from a mark. Billy played 33 times for Wales, and eight years after he retired his brother Jack came into the side and won 18 caps.

WHAT IT MIGHT COME TO
THE ABNORMAL EXTENSION OF THE
THREE QUARTER LINE

Three Doran brothers – Gerry, Bertie and Eddie – played for Ireland between 1890 and 1904. Gerry and Bertie hold the record of being the **only brothers to have scored points in international rugby in different centuries.** At Cardiff in 1970 Scotland's Gordon Brown came on the field to replace his injured elder brother Peter – the only occasion brother has taken over from brother in an international.

The Vickery family have one of the oddest father-and-son records. George played for England in 1905, and his son William played for Wales. Both were members of the Aberavon club.

Uzzell is another famous rugby name. Harry Uzzell, who won 11 caps for Wales, became the oldest man to captain Wales when he took charge in 1920 at the age of 38. Many years later, his relation John 'Dickie' Uzzell became a national figure overnight. That was in 1963, and Uzzell was a student at St Luke's College, Exeter. He sneaked out of his PE group at the college on the pretext of going to visit his sick father. Uzzell *père* was in fact heading for the grandstand at Newport to watch his son play for the home side against the All Blacks. Newport won the match 3–0, inflicting on the New Zealanders their only defeat in 34 matches, and Dickie Uzzell scored the drop-goal that caused all the commotion.

A more dubious honour was accorded Welsh internationals F. Purdon and H.M. Jordan. When Ireland arrived at Cardiff in 1884 to play Wales, they were two players short, so Purdon and Jordan were drafted into the Irish side. No accusations of treachery have survived, but it must be easier for a man who plays for two nations when he does so by his own choice.

Wells Evading the Welsh Backs

In 1921 Frank Mellish collected an extraordinary record. He played for two countries in the same year. Having won several caps for England, including appearances against Ireland and Wales in 1921, he returned to his native South Africa and in August of that year played for South Africa against New Zealand.

Then there is the strange case of Stanley Harris, who won two caps for England despite being born in South Africa. He toured South Africa with the 1924 British Lions, and was then selected by both South Africa (for boxing) and Great Britain (modern pentathlon) for the Paris Olympics. He later turned to tennis, and in 1931 played in the Davis Cup for South Africa.

While the feats of Harris bludgeon us into attitudes of awe and admiration, someone for whom there can only be heartfelt sympathy is B.I. Swanell, the Northampton and East Midlands forward, who **suffered from selectorial negligence** in his native land. Although welcomed by the British Lions, for whom he played seven times in Tests against Australia and New Zealand on the 1899 and 1904 tours, he never represented England, or even had an England trial. Swanell's reaction was to stay on in Australia after the second Lions tour, and in September 1905 he played for that country in an international against New Zealand.

Two Irishmen who successfully mixed international rugby with one other sport were F.O. Stoker and Noel Purcell. Stoker played for Ireland between 1886 and 1891 and is the only rugby international to win a tennis title at Wimbledon. In 1890, in partnership with J. Pim, he won the men's doubles. Purcell won four caps for Ireland in 1921, the year after he won an Olympic gold medal as a member of the Great Britain water polo team. In the 1924 Games he represented the independent Irish Free State and so became the first man to represent two countries in the Olympics.

The mixture of rugby with soccer is perhaps more to be expected. Scotsman H.W. Rennie-Tailyour has an early place in the record books of both sports. He played in the first international rugby match in England, the first international soccer match in England and the first FA Cup Final. He remains Scotland's only double international at rugby and soccer.

Kevin O'Flanaghan holds the unique record of playing for Ireland at rugby one Saturday, then playing soccer for Ireland against Scotland the next Saturday. He was only prevented from playing international rugby the following Saturday because fog kept him from getting to Dublin in time to turn out against England.

Despite the dazzling feats of Stanley Harris, chronicled above, our choice for the **all-time greatest all-round sportsman** is C.B. Fry. He did not achieve the highest honours at rugby, but came very close. Selected to play on the wing for Oxford in the 1895 Varsity match, he had to drop out beforehand with a pulled hamstring. Had he played, it is said that he would almost certainly have been selected for England's next match.

The injury spoiled a marvellous record for Fry. He captained England at cricket, and scored 39,886 first-class runs at an average of 50.22; he was the holder of the world long-jump record for 25 years with a leap of 23 ft 6 in; played soccer for Southampton in the 1901 Cup Final, and gained two England soccer caps. At rugby, he played for Blackheath and the Barbarians.

ENGLAND v. WALES.—A ONE-POINT VICTORY FOR ENGLAND.

JURSTON'S GREAT MARK.
THE FINEST PIECE OF DEFENSIVE PLAY IN THE MATCH.

"TWICKENHAM luck," said one of those who sit in the seats of the mighty, as he was discussing England's very fortunate win just after the match on Saturday. His hearers appreciated the point, for ever since the Rugby Union set up housekeeping at Twickenham the fickle goddess has smiled upon them. But all the good fortune they have enjoyed pales into insignificance beside the gift vouchsafed to them in the closing stages of Saturday's game, just when even the most hopeful of England's supporters were resigning themselves to apparently inevitable defeat. Surely no worse beaten side than England ever won a match. They had had all the worst of the play, and for quite two-thirds of the game had been on the defensive. Their undoubtedly brilliant three-quarters had been quite unable to get going, for the simple reason that five times out of six their forwards were beaten for possession, and their system of attack had been reduced to impotence. The only consoling feature for Englishmen was that the Welsh third line were utterly unable to make any use of the innumerable opportunities provided for them. Wales has turned out some bad three-quarter lines of late years, but this was easily the worst of the lot. Only Hirst, whose dropped goal was a real beauty, showed any signs of ability, and very rarely indeed did he get a pass. Given even one centre of average skill, not a Gwyn Nicholls or a Gabe, but an ordinarily good player, and Wales must have won handsomely.

No detailed description of the play is necessary, for it was pretty much the same thing all through. The Welsh pack, the finest I have ever seen from the Principality, dominated the whole proceedings. In the tight there was only one side in it, for the English hooker, whoever he may have been, seemed to have been stricken with the palsy, and was quite unable to obtain possession. Thanks to the senseless decision of the Rugby Union not to number the players, it was difficult to see who was doing the hooking for Wales, but I was told by those who ought to know that it was Edgar Morgan, and certainly the work was never better done. Time after time the ball came out cleanly and quickly, Lloyd would give it to C. Lewis, and the latter would, with a perseverance worthy of a better fate, in due course pass to a centre. That gentleman would then proceed to run across the ground until he was tackled or until he fell down, having meanwhile got his whole attacking force thoroughly out of position, and the movement would come to an end. C. Lewis, who is a player with brains, has been blamed for kicking too much, but having very quickly realised the weakness of the men behind him, what was he to do? Personally I thought he was almost too generous to them, for if he had left them out of the picture altogether, as R. A. Lloyd of Ireland would most certainly have done, no one could have found fault with him. It was just the kind of game that might easily have resulted in a pointless draw, for neither side ever looked really dangerous, and there was an element of luck about every one of the scores, England's first try being perhaps the least fluky of the lot. I have no wish to detract from Hirst's dropped goal, which was cleverly obtained, but even he would admit that it was from an extraordinary angle, and might not come off once in twenty shots.

The chief honours of the match go to the Welsh forwards, splendidly led by the Rev. Alban Davies, a muscular Christian if ever there was one, who worked untiringly all through, and whose strenuous tackling was the admiration of all beholders. Always prominent, too, was Uzzell, of Newport, who gave a great display in the open, and never spared himself in the scrum. The visiting pack went on the field with a splendid chance of bringing off a forlorn hope, and they very nearly did it. Enough has been said about the outsides, but Bancroft deserves mention, for he played the game we have learnt to expect from him. None too keen on tackling or stopping rushes, he is still a magnificent kick, and being assiduously fed by some of the English forwards, acting under the mistaken idea that they were dribbling, and by some of the backs as well, he had every chance given him of showing what he could do.

EIGHT MIGHTY FORWARDS.
J. BRUNTON   THE REV. ALBAN DAVIES   C. G. BROWN   P. JONES
A. T. MAYNARD   T. WILLIAMS   H. UZELL   S. SMART

The English forwards, apart from their entire inability to gain possession, did a lot of sound, hard work, and had amongst them the best forward on the ground. Brown, the old Oxford captain, did more than any other two men to win the match for England. He scored one try through being in the right place to take Poulton's pass, and he had a lot to do with the almost despairing rally that led to the winning score. Very few men, by the way, would have got over the line when he received the ball from Poulton, for he had to take two Welshmen with him, and they did not want to go. Pillman was comparatively quiet in the first half, but towards the end he got going in fine style, and if his try was lucky it was at any rate the result of persistent following up. Maynard, the Cambridge blue, made a most satisfactory first appearance for England. He was always in the van, and he is one of the few forwards of the day who can dribble. Brunton was another new-comer who did well, and Smart was very useful all through. Some of the others did not reach the same standard, and it looks as though those who wished to see the Leicester hooker included knew what they were talking about.

Wood and Taylor, not being supplied with the ball with the regularity they have learnt to expect, did not shine with their usual brilliance. They had a lot of donkey-work to do, and got through it fairly well, notwithstanding the vigorous attentions of the opposing forwards. Still, they made it pretty clear that they are more adapted for attack than for defence, and they cannot have been very pleased with themselves. Poulton was, as usual, good, bad, and indifferent. His best effort led up to Brown's try, and was cleverly conceived and carried out. His worst also led up to a try—for Wales. He kicked well at times, but was too fond of the short punt when he did get the chance of starting an attack, which was not often. His defence was stronger than of yore, but there are still holes in it. Chapman worked hard in defence, and was always difficult to hold, but he never quite got through or set Lowe in motion. The latter had a bad match; very few chances came his way, and nothing went just right for him. Watson took the popular fancy as a wholehearted trier, and it is not his fault that he just lacks the extra pace necessary for a wing. Johnston shares with Brown the honours of the day as far as England is concerned. He was steady under severe pressure, and on the only occasion on which he looked like getting into serious trouble he had plenty of time, a little peculiarity of his that has been observed before. Everything else he did was thoroughly sound, and one mark of his on his own line was among the finest bits of play ever seen. There is still only one full-back for England.

"FORWARD."

CHARGES DOWN POULTON'S PUNT, GETS POSSESSION AND RUNS IN.

PILLMAN GETS TO THE LOOSE BALL FIRST.

The history of rugby players who never quite made it to the top, or did so with extreme brevity, is long and complex, so much so that we have compiled some of the principal feats in tabular form, below.

Tourists who never got there

C.E. Murnin (Australia) Selected to tour England with the 1908 Australians. So ill on journey, had to be taken off boat and returned to Australia.

Stan Hodgson (British Lions) England and Durham City hooker. Set off on 1962 Lions tour to South Africa. Stopped over with team to play Rhodesia in Bulawayo. Broke leg. Invalided straight home.

Tourists who got there, but did not play

1939 Australian team	Reached Britain just before war declared with Germany. Went home.
Steve Smith (British Lions)	Flown out to South Africa in 1980 as replacement scrum-half for Lions. Sat on bench through last match of tour (Fourth Test). Returned home.
Bruce Malouf (Australia)	Front-row forward on his first tour to Britain (1981–82). Broke leg in training before first match. Flown home.
C.J. Van Wyk (South Africa)	Arrived in Australia on 1956 tour. Broke leg in training before first match. Flown home.
R.L. Seddon (British Lions)	Captain of first British Lions tour to Australasia (1888). Went boating on Hunter River before first match. Drowned.

Tourists who got there and played, but not for long

Stuart Lane (British Lions)	Cardiff flanker. Flew to South Africa with 1980 Lions. In first ruck of first match, against Eastern Province, emerged with torn knee ligaments. Flown home after 47 seconds of active service.
W.H. Sobey (British Lions)	Old Millhillians and England outside-half. Arrived in Australia for first game of 1930 Lions tour. Injured. Took no further part in tour.
Basil Kenyon (South Africa)	Captain of 1951–52 Springbok tour to Britain. Injured in third game of tour, against Pontypool and Newbridge. Took no further part in tour, then retired.
Douglas Smith (British Lions)	Arrived in New Zealand in 1950 with arm in plaster. Did not play until 18th game of tour. (Did better in 1971 as manager of victorious Lions).

Selected for international, but did not play

Jacques Fouroux (France)	Scrum-half. Selected for first cap v Ireland (1968). Before match, half-back partner injured, so French selectors followed tradition by dropping Fouroux and picking a new combination. (He at last got on pitch for France four years later, and went on to become captain.)
Harry Eagles (England)	Returned from 1888 Lions tour and selected for England. Game never played because England in dispute that season with other three home countries.
Wilfrid Lawry (England)	Arrived at Swansea in 1920 for first cap. Changed into match kit. Replaced at last minute because of ground conditions. (Capped later in season v France.)

Tom Stone, Harry Edwards, Charles Anderson (Wales)	Selected for first caps v Ireland (1937). Match postponed by fog, and when played later in season all three men fallen from favour and never capped.
Tommy England (Wales)	Selected for first cap v England (1890). Injured before game and replaced by new cap Billy Bancroft who played 33 consecutive matches for Wales. England retired uncapped.
H.B. Robinson, W.B. Smyth (Ireland)	Travelled to London for Ireland's first match v England in 1875 but failed to turn up at Kennington Oval. Later revealed that both came just for the trip, Robinson wanting also to visit his family. Neither invited to play for Ireland again.

Played in international, but did not touch ball

Phil Bennett (Wales)	Came on as first-ever Welsh replacement v France in 1969, with only seconds remaining. Final whistle blew. Went home.

Stepped in dramatically to play for country

André Franquenelle (France)	French sprinter. In crowd for France v Scotland game in 1911 when announced that selected centre Gaston Vareilles had disappeared. Franquenelle played superbly in France's first-ever international victory (16–15) and later won two more caps. Vareilles – who had jumped off train to buy sandwich and been left stranded – never played for France again.
Ernie Woodward (England)	Student at Trinity College, Dublin in 1880 when England team arrived with several players ill after rough sea crossing. Woodward, though unable to make Trinity 2nd XV, won his first and only cap.
Frank Thurlow Wright (England)	Law student in Edinburgh in 1881 when England team arrived minus half-back H. H. Taylor who had missed train in London. Wright, then playing for Edinburgh Academicals, captured by selectors after desperate search for an Englishman.
Unnamed coach driver and local journalist (Switzerland)	Invited to play for national XV v Bellinzona in 1977 after two players delayed by landslide. Both did so well, joined squad for next training session.

Capped only once, despite playing brilliantly

Howard Marshall
(England)

Won sole cap v Wales in 1893. Scored three tries but never selected for England again.

Chico Hopkins (Wales)

Career-long understudy to Gareth Edwards. Played once for 25 minutes v England in 1971 when Edwards injured, inspiring Wales to 17–13 victory after trailing 3–13 when he came on field.

High-scoring Lion who never played in a Test

Bob Hiller

English full-back who toured twice with Lions, scored 104 points in South Africa in 1968 but could not dislodge Tom Kiernan from Test side, then scored 102 points in New Zealand in 1971 when J.P.R. Williams was Test full-back.

Capped only once, but quite satisfied

Bert Solomon (England)

Played well in début v Wales in 1910, then declined all further offers of caps, saying happy enough playing solely for Redruth.

Capped in error, but did not complain

Arnold Alcock (England)

Average Blackheath player, amazed to receive letter inviting him to play for England v South Africa in 1906. England secretary equally surprised to see Alcock reporting for game, since letter should have been sent to Andrew Slocock. Too late to change team, so Alcock played.

BIZARRE RULES

AND

RULINGS

MOST PRIMITIVE LAWS

By 1863 football was divided into two schools. One was led by the Etonians, who preferred the dribbling game and wished to outlaw handling, mauling and hacking. This they had achieved at a meeting at Cambridge in 1846, where a breakaway code of 'Cambridge Rules' was agreed – which later formed the basis of the Football Association's rules when that body was founded in 1863.

Clubs in favour of handling and hacking also had a significant meeting in London in 1863, at which it was confirmed that 'a player may be hacked on the front of the leg below the knee whilst running with the ball'. Opponents were also allowed to trip the player with the ball, but him only. Members of the Blackheath club thought this was verging on softness, and they withdrew from the association of 11 clubs. Over the next decade the mood changed as a growing number of clubs (including Blackheath) sought to develop a more fluid rugby football game in place of the customary physical battle of attrition centred on a gigantic scrum from which the ball seldom emerged. By 1878 the Rugby Football Union (formed in 1871) was sufficiently concerned about danger to the person to declare that 'No-one wearing projecting nails, iron plates and gutta percha on any part of his boots should be allowed to play.' Gutta percha was a hard flexible gum recently imported from Asia which did better service, principally in Scotland to begin with, as the 'guttie' golf ball. There was now no place for it in the newly gentrified game of Rugby Union.

KNOCK-OUT KINGS

At the turn of the century the Badminton Library's volume on *Football*, in its Sports and Pastimes series, spoke of Scottish rugby as a 'game of the classes; the masses are devoted to Association...' The only place where this did not apply was in the Borders, already famous as the region which invented Sevens.

This apparently came about in 1883, when the Melrose club hit a financially sticky patch. Local butcher Ned Haig determined to help out the club by organizing a seven-a-side tournament. It was an immediate success, and the following year Gala launched their own tournament with six teams competing for the championship.

A century later, one of the seven-a-side game's less well-known laws surfaced in the Army tournament held at Aldershot on 3 May 1984. Five minutes after the start of the final, between the Welsh Guards and the Royal Horse Artillery, the captains, managers and referee were called to a touchline conference. The Welsh Guards were told that one of their players, Steve Whitehouse, was ineligible because he had been injured in a previous round. Whitehouse had already scored two tries and his side were leading 8–0. The game was replayed and the Welsh Guards then beat their opponents 18–16 with a new player, Ian Edwards.

MOST PENALTY-FREE MATCH

In November 1979, in Toulon, France, a team from HMS *Ajax* and one from HMS *Scylla* had to play a match on a soccer pitch because no-one had thought to book a rugby ground. This called for certain amendments to the laws. Because of the height of the crossbar the teams agreed that no penalties were to be kicked at goal, and there were to be no conversion attempts; drop-goals, on the other hand, would count. Drop-outs were taken from the edge of the penalty area. HMS *Scylla* seem to have acclimatized more quickly to the new rules, winning the match 16–14.

MOST LINGERING SUDDEN DEATH

In the 1982–83 championship third-place play-off match between Californian clubs Monterey and Fresno, the rules were straightforward. The game was to commence at 10 am, and would consist of two 30-minute halves and a five-minute half-time interval. The captains and referee agreed that if the match was tied at full-time they would go into 'sudden death' overtime.

The score at full-time was 13–13. The weather was cold and rainy, but the teams played on…and on…and on. Monterey eventually scored a try to win the match 17–13. 'Sudden death' had lasted 150 minutes. Spare a thought, finally, for referee Dan Hickey who had to return an hour later to take charge of the final!

FIRST SHOOT-OUT

The first major 'shoot-out' occurred at the 1984 French championship final. At full-time Béziers and Agen were level at 15–15. A replay was out of the question because many of the players had to fly to New Zealand with the French national team immediately afterwards. So they played extra-time. The score moved on to 21–21. The next solution was a soccer-style penalty competition, with selected players taking penalties from the 22-metre line. Béziers eventually won 21–21, and 3–1 on penalties.

FIT
FOR
NOTHING

Life in the front row is rough enough already, without extra training. That was
evidently the view of one Surrey prop in the early 1970s when Bob Hiller, as county
captain, introduced a series of **punishing exercises** in the changing-room before
the teams took the field. Murray, the Harlequins prop, was so exhausted after one
of these sessions that he was heard to mutter: 'Can I have my orange now?'

Phil O'Callaghan, the Irish international prop, doubted that a slice of fruit would be enough to revive him at half-time. In 1975 he came on the field as a substitute when Ireland played the President's XV at Lansdowne Road as part of the Irish Centenary celebrations. In his first scrum, a packet of cigarettes and a lighter fell out of O'Callaghan's pocket. In a flash, he broke up the scrum and handed the cigarettes and lighter to Norman Sansom, the referee. 'Hold these until half-time,' he said, 'I'm not too keen on oranges.'

Asked in June 1982 what he thought of the England rugby team's suitability for American Football, Bob Ward, coach of the Dallas Cowboys, produced this wonderful backhanded compliment:

'They were remarkably fit, agile, strong and fast, and if ever a **league was opened for dwarfs**, they would be national champions. Woodward and Swift would make excellent line receivers if they put on four stones in weight. Wheeler and Blakeway would be perfect linemen if they were just eight inches taller. Steve Bainbridge was the right height – 6 ft 6 in – but was five stones too light. Dusty Hare, though, could make the grade as a kicker.'

How to carry your manager: John Dawes, captain of the 1971 Lions, struggles with the administrative burden of Dr D. Smith.

Nuns instruct would-be Wallabies in the finer points of scrummaging at a Roman Catholic school in Bowral, Australia.

The whole secret of training is not to take things too far. This was the undoing of Jaco Reinach, the right wing for Orange Free State. Reinach should certainly have known better because he was also the South African 400 metres record-holder, at 45.01 seconds. Despite this, Reinach decided to get fit for the 1984 season by entering the Free State triathlon. This consists of a 500 metre swim, a 10 km cycle ride followed by a 10 km run.

Reinach, being a complete non-swimmer, attempted to struggle through the 500 metre swim with a pair of water wings. Unfortunately, after 300 metres, the **water wings punctured** and Reinach, in desperate trouble, was hauled by his team-mates to safety.

Looks can deceive, in rugby as in other matters. If a player is an odd shape, it is all too easy to rate him as useless. A tall, gangling Number 8 joined London Welsh at the start of the 1968–69 season from Old Guildfordians. The first team were not winning much ball at the back of the line-out, and captain John Dawes asked the selection committee whether anyone in the junior teams might be worth a try. This was the assessment he got from one of the selectors, Glan Richards: 'Well, there's this lad Mervyn Davies in the 3rd XV. He may win you some line-out ball but he **won't do much else**.'

Mervyn Davies played his first game for London Welsh on 2 November, and on 1 February played his first game for Wales. He played 38 consecutive games for Wales, and was rated as the finest Number 8 world rugby has seen.

The game was in its infancy in Ireland when the 1881 team inspired this description by J. J. McCarthy: 'Ten men from the North and ten from the South were nominated to play England next February. Of those who turned up – and some simply didn't – one half were complete strangers to each other. The whole lot were **immaculately innocent of training...**'

Top. The agony of sit-ups: Paul Dodge, assisted by The Invisible Bulk, on the 1980 Lions tour of South Africa.
Bottom. Worm's eye-view of the Welsh pack in training, at Twickenham in 1968.

BIZARRE REFEREEING RECORDS

MOST AND LEAST SHARP-SIGHTED REFEREES

Praise, at last, for the man with the whistle. Admittedly, the incident took place 53 years ago, but never mind. When the half-time whistle blew at the England v Wales games at Twickenham in 1931, the score was 6–6. Before the game restarted, England had taken an 8–6 lead. The reason for the change was that when England scored a try at the end of the first half, neither touch-judge had raised his flag for the conversion. The referee, however, was in a position to rule that the conversion had been made and ordered the score to be changed. The match ended in an 11–11 draw.

Abuse, on the other hand, is almost certain to follow a controversial decision. Irish referee John West, who refused a try to Wales against England at Twickenham in 1974 – a match which England won 16–12 – became the butt of a series of Welsh jokes, to which Max Boyce contributed with a song about blind Irish referees. Two years later, when he was in Cardiff for the Wales v France game, the local Referees Society invited him to be their guest of honour. Mr West, a fine international referee and a good humourist, was presented with a copy of Boyce's record, and a white stick.

MOST DISMISSIVE REFEREE

In December 1982 referee Peter Richmond sent off all 30 players in the Abingdon v Didcot match. All 30 were suspended for 30 days. The referee's comment was: 'They didn't seem to be too interested in wanting to play rugby.'

MOST GENTLEMANLY REFEREE

Roy Veitch, a former Jedforest player and a local referee, struck a blow for all those who deplore the soccer-style kissing and cuddling which is creeping into rugby. He was refereeing a Colts game at Dumfries when a centre-threequarter was mobbed by his team-mates after scoring a try. Mr Veitch allowed the conversion attempt, then penalized the scoring team by awarding a penalty to the opposition on the grounds that Dumfries had infringed Law 26, relating to ungentlemanly conduct.

MOST (UN) BALANCED REFEREE

Two wrongs *can* make a right, and it took a rugby referee to prove it. When Ireland beat Wales 9–6 in Dublin in 1968, the scoreline included two drop-goals that should never have been given. The first, by Gareth Edwards, sailed comfortably wide of the target, and then Mike Gibson replied in kind with an effort that took a huge deflection off a Welsh player, which in those days should have invalidated the kick. Instead, it invalidated the previous gift to the Welshmen.

THE ONLY APPARENT WAY OF BEATING THE NEW ZEALANDERS
A REFEREE WHO WILL WHISTLE WHENEVER AN 'ALL BLACK' IS ABOUT TO SCORE

MOST HYGIENIC REFEREE

For their first-round match in the Natal Cup in 1983, Tembu had to travel to the black protectorate of Transkei to play Ciskei RFC. When they arrived they found that they had brought 15 shirts but only 12 pairs of shorts. The referee refused to allow the three under-equipped players to take the field in their underpants, so they had to sit on the touchline and watch their side go out of the Cup by 24 points to 6!

LEAST MOBILE REFEREE

The crowd always get excited if the referee goes down injured, and it usually requires the sight of a stretcher coming on the field to modify the whistles and raucous laughter. Two recent sufferers at international level were the French referee Monsieur Calmet, who in 1970 collided with one of the English forwards in the match against Wales and was later found to have suffered a broken leg. Three years later, English referee Ken Pattison was injured and had to leave the field during the France v Scotland game at Parc des Princes.

In both instances, an able replacement took charge for the rest of the match. It is not always so. One of the greatest refereeing disasters of the modern era was the performance of Doctor André Cuny of France in the Scotland v Wales game at Cardiff in 1976.

Dr Cuny severely pulled a calf muscle after a collision with one of the players, but insisted on continuing despite being unable to get closer than thirty yards to virtually every ruck and maul; these soon developed into free-for-alls. Although he had two international referees as touch-judges, the Doctor insisted that, since he could see perfectly, he would continue. Aged 48 at the time, he was refereeing his first international. It was also his last.

MOST ABSENT-MINDED REFEREE

In the 1950s the great All Black full-back George Nepia was still taking part in charity matches. In one of them he scored a unique try. The ball came straight to him after a clearance, he saw a gap in the defence, and went straight through to score under the posts. What made it unique was that he was the referee at the time!

MOST REDUNDANT REFEREE

In the 1981–82 season two Birkenhead sides, both possessing long unbeaten records, met on the coldest day of that winter. Skilful rugby was made impossible by a freezing wind and poor ground conditions. Stoppages for injuries, fighting and cautions were hideously regular. Shivering players must have doubted the match would ever end. Officially it didn't. With about 12 minutes remaining, the score was 3–3. As the referee admonished the packs yet again, both captains simultaneously called for three cheers for the referee. Both teams departed, leaving the referee bemused and jobless.

MOST DANGEROUS REFEREE

The obverse of the wounded ref is the one who starts laying into the players. The Melbourne Harlequins Under-20 hooker, Steve Hanlon, claims to be the only player ever to have been knocked out by a referee. In a game against Melbourne University, which the Harlequins won by 60 points to 3, the referee whistled for an offside decision. His flamboyant arm signal was intercepted by Hanlon who ran straight into the referee's outstretched fist, and was laid unconscious.

Spottiest match official, recorded at Westport, New Zealand.

MOST EMBARRASSED OFFICIAL

The New Zealand Maoris team which toured Britain in 1889–90 played no fewer than 74 matches; the only 'trouble' came in the match against Yorkshire. Mr Cail, the referee, was horrified to discover that his watch had stopped and immediately brought the match to a halt. As a contemporary observer described the next minutes: 'The crowd were treated to the sight of the referee coming up to the Press Stand and pathetically appealing for information as regarded the time. No less amusing were the various and different replies made by the pressmen and adjoining spectators...'

BIGGEST ROBOT

The pattern of things to come? When England played the Mid-West in Chicago on their 1982 tour of America they were astonished when the referee blew for a supposed infringement during a three-quarter movement. Querying the decision, the England team were told by the referee that the match was sponsored by the local television station and that at suitable intervals they had to stop for commercial breaks. Said the referee: 'I wore a bleeper. Three bleeps and I had to stop for precisely one minute.'

MOST UNWELCOME REFEREE

It is part of the referee's burden to expect insults while on the field of play – but even more insulting to be barred from getting on the pitch in the first place. This was the unfortunate lot of famous international referee Cyril Gadney, when he turned up to officiate at the Wales v Ireland game in 1936. Wales were in line for the championship and Ireland for the triple crown, and interest in the game was high. When Gadney arrived at the ground he was told that he was not the first person who had tried to get in by claiming he was the referee, so would he kindly clear off. Welsh officials eventually came to his rescue and escorted him into the ground.

DONT
SHOOT
❦ *THE* ❦
SECRETARY

In 1983, members of Warlingham 5th XV were on their way to play their great rivals from Old Croydonians. Their fleet of cars passed that of their opponents near the A23, and the normal statutory signals were passed. A couple of minutes later, it dawned on the more responsible members of the side that both teams had presumed they were playing away from home! Both fleets hastily turned round and passed each other going at 40 mph in the opposite direction! A third passing movement terminated in a layby where a solution was negotiated.

      A familiar scenario? Perhaps, but finding out which match secretary had got it wrong is usually impossible to establish. Even when you have got your man **blindfolded against a wall** and puffing on his last cigarette, he will still protest out of the corner of his mouth that it was the other guy's fault. Nine times out of ten he will win a last-minute reprieve, because he knows that no match secretary worth his salt ever keeps incriminating correspondence. The only way he is likely to be caught is if his opposite number is a real idiot and can produce a document justifying his team's journey, whereas he himself did the conventional thing and burnt all his letters as soon as he had roughed out that season's fixture list. Only then can the finger of guilt swing in his direction.

For up-and-coming secretaries another important thing to remember is: **commit your cock-ups in style**. For example, when Mombasa RFC travelled to Nairobi in 1974 to play against one of the local Harlequin teams, they flew the 475 miles and arrived in Nairobi in an hour and a half. Meanwhile, 30,000 feet below their aeroplane, the Harlequin lads were doggedly making the journey to Mombasa in a fleet of cars. Now, because of the aforementioned difficulty in deciding whose fault it was, we cannot for certain pin anything on the Mombasa secretary. On the other hand, how much safer he must have felt than the secretary of the Harlequins, who had subjected his lads to a bum-numbing two-way trek of 950 miles.

It is difficult to imagine that sort of thing happening to an Irish team, but in 1975 it did. The national side, on their way back from New Zealand during their Centenary year, stopped over in Fiji. On landing at Suva airport, they were a little surprised to find no welcoming committee. It was later explained that the Fijian officials were with the rest of the team on a full-scale tour of Australia!

A refinement of secretarial blundering is to get both teams to the same ground at the same time – and then have them change into identical strip. In colonial East Africa rugby was very popular just before the Second World War. Uganda, who in those days played in white, were hosts to the Kenyan national side, who also turned up in white. No spare shirts were available and it looked as though the match would have to be abandoned when a resourceful lady (surely not the secretary's wife?) produced some dye and a bucket of water. The Ugandan shirts were dipped in the bucket, and were still drying when the players took the field. Black remains the national colour.

Minor officials sometimes make the mistake of thinking that their secretary is a **near-relation of the Almighty** . When Prince Charles came to watch the Wales v Ireland game in 1969 he was inevitably caught up in the crowds and the then secretary, Bill Clement, gave instructions to his stewards to report to him as soon as the honoured guest had arrived. When the entourage finally appeared, an eager steward leapt up, pulled the car door open and said to Prince Charles: 'Hurry up, you're in dead trouble, Mr Clement's been waiting for you for half an hour!'

Perhaps the **entire committee should have been shot** when it was announced that Sydney RFC had decided to erase from the *Guinness Book of Records* the name of Barberton RFC, South Africa, for having the world's tallest rugby posts. Barberton's posts were 95 ft high. At a cost of £4000, the Sydney club imported posts of 105 ft from the Argentine. Unfortunately, they had failed to allow any extra for the holes needed to secure the posts. When the uprights were sunk the necessary 12 ft, they were only 93 ft above ground and so Barberton retained their place in the record books. (This record has since passed to the Roan Antelope club of Luanshya in Zambia, whose posts are 110 ft 6 in high.)

HEROES

& — A N D —

VILLAINS

First the heroes. Unfortunately, only two have been presented for selection, and they are both Welshmen. No matter; both tales clearly show how generously the Welsh people look after their great sportsmen.

Gareth Edwards left a reception but got no further than the car park, where he found that the lights on his car had fused. His response was to ring the police and explain his difficulty. The police understandingly sent round two squad cars and escorted Edwards home to Porthcawl – one police car in front, followed by Edwards minus lights, with the second police car bringing up the rear.

One of the legendary stories – true or otherwise – concerns Keith Jarrett, the nineteen-year-old who played for Wales against England in 1967 and, on his début, scored 19 points in Wales's win by 34 points to 21.

Jarrett, who lived in and played for Newport, returned after the celebrations to Cardiff Bus Garage. The last bus had gone. It was eight miles to Newport.

Luckily, one of the drivers recognized Jarrett from his deeds that afternoon. He offered him a lift home in one of the buses. Driving out of the garage, with Jarrett the sole passenger, the driver passed his inspector.

'What the hell are you doing?'

'Taking Mr Jarrett home, he just scored 19 points against England.'

The inspector looked through the window, saw Jarrett, then turned on the bus driver. 'You fool!' he cried. 'Go back and get a double-decker. The lad might want to smoke.'

Now the villains, who are in much greater supply. The author of *The*

Theory of Modern Rugby Football (1930) adequately described the kind of villain we mean when he wrote: 'Recently, a well-known international in his book on Rugby said that a gentleman kicks another with his instep instead of with the toe of his boot. A man who kicks another intentionally is a **blackguard and a coward.'**

Five years before those words were published, on 25 January 1925 Cyril Brownlie of New Zealand became the first player to be sent off in an international and the first player to be sent off at Twickenham. Despite the shock of being reduced to 14 men, New Zealand still managed to beat England.

Another New Zealander to distinguish himself for villainy was the anyway legendary Colin Meads. In December 1967 he was sent off against Scotland at Murrayfield for lunging with his foot as David Chisholm was about to play the ball. Meads had already been warned for dangerous play.

EXCESSIVE APPLICATION
OF THE ART OF "HEELING OUT"

The first Lion to be sent off in modern times was John O'Shea, dismissed while the Lions were beating Eastern Transvaal 37–9 in 1968. The first players to be sent off in an international championship game were Geoff Wheel (Wales) and Willie Duggan (Ireland). The referee was Norman Sansom and both men got their marching orders from the same incident. The match was played at Cardiff in January 1977 and Wales won 25–9.

All Black Keith Murdoch had a rough and controversial tour in 1972, which ended after a fracas with security guards following the banquet intended to celebrate the Wales v New Zealand game. This was Murdoch's last chance and he was sent home – or at least in the general direction of home. The sacked prop was evidently so worried about the reception he would get in New Zealand that he drifted around the outback of Western Australia for more than sixteen months before he dared to complete his journey.

Sometimes the police get it right, and sometimes they don't. Members of Hoylake RFC felt hard done by when police arrested their prop-forward Kenneth

Roberts at half-time during a match against Birkenhead Park. Roberts was removed for non-payment of motoring fines and that evening he was still **locked in a police cell wearing his rugby kit.** Hoylake, who had been leading 9–0 at half-time despite the previous loss of another player through injury, ended the match 10–9 losers. Among Hoylake partisans it became difficult to ignore the fact that they had only recently thumped the local police team 38–12.

Paul Knee, the Warwickshire and Coventry winger, was stopped by police whilst pedalling round country lanes near his home in an attempt to regain fitness after an injury. The police were searching for two armed robbers, one wearing a blue track-suit similar to Knee's, who had crashed a getaway car in the area while on the run from Oxford. Knee was only **released after a severe grilling** because he managed to convince the police of his knowledge of the area around the village of Wolston, where he lived.

Chaos and all-round villainy are part of rugby life in Argentina. In 1980, for example, in the 552 matches played in the First Division championship, no fewer than 251 players were sent off. It took the disciplinary committee until January 1984 to sentence all the culprits.

It isn't always what a man does on the pitch that puts him in the doghouse. In the 1950s the Nile RFC had a promising black player who was something of an embarrassment. He played well enough, and was selected as a reserve for East Africa against the 1955 Lions. The problem was that he was the only black member of the 1st XV, and in those days (before any Winds of Change had blown) a bit of a social outcast. He used to sit outside the clubhouse after matches drinking Coke, and it was only when a touring team from Nairobi Nondescripts asked why he was hanging around outside that he was invited into the bar. His name: Idi Amin.

MOST
FANATICAL
SUPPORTERS

Welsh Rare Bit, glimpsed at Twickenham.

Welsh rugby supporters take
a lot of beating when it comes to turning out in force in
all weathers. Not surprisingly, a Welsh crowd holds the attendance record for a
British club match: 48,500 spectators were at Cardiff Arms Park on 17 February
1951 to see Newport beat Cardiff 8–3. This turnout was also higher than for any
Football League match played in Britain that day.

       Individual Welshmen also have their moments. One weekend that
Gareth Taylor is unlikely to forget happened in February 1984, when he travelled
from Cologne to Paris to watch the France v Wales game, only to find that it was due
to be played in Cardiff. Mr Taylor stayed on to watch a friendly soccer match
between the French First Division team Paris St Germain and the Brazilians
Fluminense. He was glad he stayed because at half-time he won £475 in the
programme lottery.

       A new era in Welsh fanaticism can be said to have dawned on 23
January 1982, the début of the red dragon which walked on to the pitch during the
Ireland v Wales match. When cautioned, the dragon explained that he felt he would
be more use on the field than off it. 'Besides,' he said, with unfathomable logic, 'I'm
prettier than that Bill Beaumont.'

That evening, the dragon presented himself at the door of a night club. He was looking very smart with his bright red body, gleaming horns and fierce teeth. His tail brushed the ground. Unfortunately the dragon (also identifiable as one Edward Prosser from Porth Glamorgan) found his path blocked by a massive doorman an inch or two taller than Willie John McBride.

'Why can't I come in?' he asked.

'Because we don't serve dragons,' said the doorman.

'Just one drink,' said the dragon.

'Not even one,' replied the doorman.

The dragon stamped his paw and wandered off into the night. A fortnight later he would turn up in London, his first major appearance being in front of Hammersmith magistrates where he was charged with being drunk and disorderly before the England v Wales game. Defending himself against allegations that he had 'leaked' in public, the dragon said:

'It was a wrongful arrest because I am a dragon, and where else can we do these things?'

114

The courtroom burst into laughter, but the dragon was found guilty and fined £10. When asked if he had anything further to say, he complained: 'I was given the wrong breakfast. I should have had coal and a box of firelighters, and all I got was egg on toast.'

'I don't know why they were picking on me,' he added later. 'There were fifteen of us doing it. I don't think I was particularly conspicuous.'

Cardiff was the venue for a remarkable feat of endurance by the fans who waited some three hours on a hot afternoon for the home club's match against Coventry to begin. Still more remarkable was the feat of the St Alban Silver Band, who took up their position on the field of play shortly before 2.30.

News had already reached Cardiff that the Coventry coach had broken down at Usk. The band began to play, and they were still playing when further news came through that the replacement coach had conked out some miles short of the rescue area. Five cars were dispatched to Usk to collect the Coventry team; four got there. The band played on.

At 5.15 the match began. Astonishingly, only one man, a cornet player, was seen breaking ranks in the course of a **165-minute concert in which no tune was repeated.** The match was also good value, finishing in a 25–25 draw.

Things are not always as they may seem. That was the experience of the Llanelli supporter who was having an amiable conversation with two Wasps fans, one male and one female, during the 1983–84 match at Stradey Park. Just after half-time, with the score 7-all, Llanelli had a storming ten-minute period in which they scored three tries, reducing the Wasps supporters to glum silence. The Welshman could not let this go unnoticed so he tapped the woman on the shoulder and said: 'Your husband has gone very quiet.'

'He ought to be,' answered the woman, 'he's been dead for two years!'

On the subject of female supporters, it is **not widely known that Princess Christina of Schleswig-Holstein is extremely keen on rugby.** In 1956 the organizers of the Hospitals Cup Final, between Guys and St Mary's, were delighted when it was announced that she would be attending the match. She arrived with her entourage, and was wined and dined by the President of the United Hospitals, and eventually left in her Rolls Royce after the match had finished in a 3–3 draw. It was only after an official invitation had been extended for her to attend the replay (which St Mary's won 16–0) that it was discovered that the Royal visitors were in fact a group of students from Guys Hospital.

Team mascots come in two varieties – live and manufactured. One of the most celebrated mascots in the latter group was a substitute British Lion which travelled to the other side of the world in a classic 'mercy dash' which ended in what can only be classed as **magnificent failure.** The mascot was the creation of a Cheshire shirt company who presented it to the 1977 British Lions for their tour of New Zealand. Shortly before the final Test, the four-foot-long mascot was stolen from the team bus.

On hearing the news, the managing director of the shirt company, John Keeley, went in search of an identical one, which he had given to an oil company director. He, however, had passed it on to his cleaner, and this bewildered lady had to be hastily relieved of her present. The lion was then flown to New Zealand and arrived in Auckland just in time for the kick-off. The Lions lost the Test 10–9, and with it the series…

Probably the most unusual live mascot carried around by a touring side was a snake which the 1909 Australians brought with them to Britain. Before their game against Llanelli the snake died – and the tourists suffered their first defeat of the tour.

In 1975 a member of Pontoise RFC, Paris, was stopped by Customs at Dover and charged with flouting the quarantine laws which forbid the import of live animals – in this case a cockerel, the French emblem. He explained that he was on his way to the international at Twickenham and was going to present it to the people he was staying with over the weekend, as a gift for their hospitality.

This was not the only *coq* to make the cross-Channel trip in 1975. A chambermaid in a London Bridge hotel had to be taken to hospital suffering from shock after a **live cockerel accelerated out of a wardrobe** in her direction as she began her chores on the Monday morning after the game.

Is streaking an act of support? If so, it is certainly extreme, and therefore comes into the category of fanatical. It can be argued, on the other hand, that streaking is mere exhibitionism and has little to do with the event at which it is committed. Our findings incline to the view that most streakers are first and foremost sports fans, and that the urge to strip off only attacks them on rare and special occasions.

The **first recorded sports streaker** ran on the field at Bedford Town FC at half-time on 9 March 1974. A fortnight later an Australian, Michael O'Brien, became the first streaker to be arrested at a rugby international – the match between England and France at Twickenham. A police helmet was placed over the offending parts and this helmet, together with the award-winning press photograph which features it, is on display at the Rugby Club in Hallam Street, London W1.

Portrait of a Nude Full-back, streaking into the line at Lansdowne Road, Dublin.

Many were the comments made both during and after Erika Roe's famous streak at half-time in the 1982 international between England and Australia:

England's captain, Bill Beaumont: 'Three times I tried to get the lads' attention for the half-time pep talk, but they would keep turning round.'

Erika's employer, Mr Frank Westwood: 'She should have been in the office.' And: 'I didn't recognize her on television.'

Erika's father, Mr Peter Roe: 'She spent her childhood in Africa, where such things are not regarded with disfavour. It is seen as being perfectly natural.' And: 'I first saw the incident on the News. It was a lovely picture. She had her arms out – **just like the Pope.'**

Sarah Bennett, co-streaker: 'How come she got all the publicity?'

To commemorate her bold deed, Erika made a record which was released in December 1982, sold 23 copies and was hailed as the Worst Record of the Year. Oh, well… shame about the voice.

The Morning After.

PHOTO ACKNOWLEDGMENTS

The publishers thank the following sources
for their help in providing illustrations:
Dave Cannon/Allsport Photographic, Central Press,
Tony Duffy/Allsport Photographic, Fox Photos,
Illustrated London News Picture Library, Keystone,
Adrian Murrell/Allsport Photographic,
Mike Powell/Allsport Photographic, Sydney Morning Herald